C000229883

How to Look Good in a W

HOW TO LOOK GOOD IN A WAR

Justifying and Challenging State Violence

Brian Rappert

PlutoPress
www.plutobooks.com

First published 2012 by Pluto Press
345 Archway Road, London N6 5AA

www.plutobooks.com

Distributed in the United States of America exclusively by
Palgrave Macmillan, a division of St. Martin's Press LLC,
175 Fifth Avenue, New York, NY 10010

British Library Cataloguing in Publication Data
A catalogue record for this book is available from the British Library

ISBN   978 0 7453 3180 5   Hardback
ISBN   978 0 7453 3179 9   Paperback
ISBN   978 1 8496 4773 1   PDF eBook
ISBN   978 1 8496 4775 5   Kindle eBook
ISBN   978 1 8496 4774 8   EPUB eBook

Library of Congress Cataloging in Publication Data applied for

This book is printed on paper suitable for recycling and made from fully managed
and sustained forest sources. Logging, pulping and manufacturing processes are
expected to conform to the environmental standards of the country of origin.

10   9   8   7   6   5   4   3   2   1

Designed and produced for Pluto Press by Chase Publishing Services Ltd
Typeset from disk by Stanford DTP Services, Northampton, England
Simultaneously printed digitally by CPI Antony Rowe, Chippenham, UK and
Edwards Bros in the United States of America

Contents

Abbreviations

APM	Anti-personnel mines
BBC	British Broadcasting Corporation
BTWC	Biological and Toxin Weapons Convention
CCM	Convention on Cluster Munitions
CCW	Convention on Certain Conventional Weapons
CIA	Central Intelligence Agency
CMC	Cluster Munition Coalition
CWC	Chemical Weapons Convention
DfID	Department for International Development
DIME	Dense inert metal explosives
EU	European Union
FCO	Foreign and Commonwealth Office (UK)
FoI	Freedom of information
ISC	Intelligence and Security Committee (UK)
ICRC	International Committee of the Red Cross
IHL	International humanitarian law
IRI	International Republican Institute
JIC	Joint Intelligence Committee
MoD	Ministry of Defence (UK)
MoH	Ministry of Health (Iraq)
MP	Member of Parliament
NATO	North Atlantic Treaty Organization
NGO	Non-governmental organization
NPT	Treaty on the Non-Proliferation of Nuclear Weapons
R&D	Research and development
US	United States of America
UK	United Kingdom
UN	United Nations
WHO	World Health Organization
WMD	Weapons of mass destruction

Preface

This book is the product of over ten years of engagement with efforts to limit the humanitarian harms of conflict. That path began with a chance opportunity to take part in the Amnesty International (UK) Working Group on the Arms and Security Trade. Since then, my thinking and practice has benefited from experiences with many individuals and organizations.

The work conducted for this book could not have been undertaken without the assistance of many people. My particular thanks to Brian Balmer, Eitan Barak, Carole Boudeau, John Borrie, Maya Brehm, Robin Collins, Catelijne Coopmans, Simon Conway, Stuart Croft, Bonnie Docherty, Malcolm Dando, Chandré Gould, Alastair Hay, Peter Herby, Iain Lang, Susan Maret, Brian Martin, Linsey McGoey, Thomas Nash, Kathryn Nixdorff, 'A.N. Other', Margarita Petrova, Elvira Rosert, Ben Rusek, Ken Rutherford, Andy Stirling, Seb Taylor, Susanne Weber, Virgil Wiebe, Steve Woolgar, and Steve Wright. A special thanks to Giovanna Colombetti for, well, so much. A special thanks to Richard Moyes as well. I have had the good fortune to work closely with several inspiring people over the course of my career. Richard has been a steadfast colleague and friend in investigating the machinations of statecraft.

How to Look Good in a War has been informed by work undertaken with disarmament and human rights groups such as Action on Armed Violence, Cluster Munitions Coalition, Landmine Action, and Pax Christi (Netherlands). I conducted dozens of presentations related to the themes of this book, at forums such as the Biological Weapons Convention, the Certain Conventional Weapons Convention, the Oslo Process, and the UNIDIR's Discourse on Explosive Weapons Project. My thanks to all those that participated in these events.

Sections of the book are reworked reformulations of parts of earlier publications. Kind permission was given by John Benjamins Publishing Company Amsterdam/Philadelphia for drawing on elements of Brian Rappert, (2011) 'The Language of Judgement, Spin, and Accountability' *Journal of Language and Politics* 10(2): 182–203; the Taylor and Francis Group for elements of Brian Rappert and Richard Moyes (2010) 'Enhancing the Protection of Civilians from Armed Conflict: Precautionary Lessons' *Medicine, Conflict & Survival* 26(1) January–March: 24–47, and Brian Rappert (2012) 'States of Ignorance: The Unmaking and Remaking of Death Tolls' *Economy and Society* 41(1): 42–63; Emerald Group Publishing Limited for elements of Brian Rappert, Richard Moyes, and A.N. Other (2011) 'Statecrafting Ignorance: Strategies for Managing Burdens, Secrecy, and Conflict' in S. Maret (ed.) *Government Secrecy* (*Research in Social Problems and Public Policy*, Volume 19) London: Emerald: 301–324 and Landmine Action for elements of Brian Rappert (2008) *A Convention beyond the Convention: Stigma, Humanitarian Standards, and the Oslo Process*, London: Landmine Action.

Introduction: Grasping Shadows

The scene: On November 17, 2004, the British Foreign Secretary Jack Straw stood before the House of Commons to offer a latest statement on the conflict in Iraq. As with so many others, this one was given at a time of turmoil. Continuing attacks by insurgents and terrorists, the recent US siege of Falluja, and the extensive fighting in Najaf were just some of the events casting doubt on the security situation in the country.

Argument 1: Against concerns about deaths to civilians resulting from UK and US Coalition forces, the Foreign Secretary sought to reassure those listening:

> The basic obligations under international humanitarian law as regards civilian casualties in an armed conflict are set out in additional protocol 1 to the Geneva conventions ... In particular, indiscriminate attacks are prohibited, and this includes any
>
> > '*attack which may be expected to cause incidental loss of civilian life, injury to civilians, damage to civilian objects, or a combination thereof, which would be excessive in relation to the concrete and direct military advantage anticipated*'.
>
> This obligation under international humanitarian law has been fully complied with by the United Kingdom in respect of all military operations in Iraq.[1]

This assurance was being offered specifically in response to a study that appeared in the medical journal *The Lancet* estimating some 98,000 more Iraqis had died since the start of the war than would have in the absence of it.[2]

Argument 2: Straw responded to this study, not by offering an official British number, but rather by countering the suggestion that any estimation was feasible at all. As he said, 'In many cases it would be impossible to make a reliably accurate assessment either of the civilian casualties resulting from any particular attacks or of the overall civilian casualties of a conflict. This is particularly true in the conditions that exist in Iraq'.[3]

Taken together, these two arguments formed a rather curious stance: on the one hand, it was stated that the UK was entirely complying with its international obligations to ensure attacks would not cause civilian harm in excess of their military advantage. On the other hand, and in almost the same breath, it was said that it was not possible for the British government (or anyone else) to determine civilian casualties reliably.

More curious still was how the notion of 'reliable' was subsequently characterized in his statement.

Argument 3: While Straw said it was 'impossible to make a reliably accurate assessment of civilian casualties', he also contended that the hospital reports compiled by the Iraqi Ministry of Health – indicating that there were 3,853 *civilian fatalities* from the military or terrorist actions between April 5, 2004 and October 5, 2004 – were the 'most reliable available' figures.

So it was both impossible to derive reliable tallies and possible to specify the most trustworthy ones.

Although the Foreign Secretary seemed not to recognize any friction between these parts of his statement, it is possible to identify some: How could international humanitarian law have been adhered to in the absence of the information about the consequences from UK military actions? Was the UK arguing that its obligation to avoid attacks that 'may be *expected*' to cause disproportionate harm meant it did not have to gauge its actual battlefield experience? What did it imply for the standing of the law if, amid decries of suffering, a senior minister could declare it had been fully complied with while also openly admitting it was not possible to do what was called for by the law? Was there, perhaps, some unspoken detail or coded significance in his statement that could unlock what was really said? What, precisely, did the term 'reliable' mean anyway?

With regard to Iraqi deaths, this is just the start of questioning. As examined in Chapter 2, subsequent press leaks and freedom of information (FoI) requests gave grounds for distrusting the doubt expressed by Straw. These suggested that, behind the scenes, civil servants were seeking to foment ignorance about Iraqi civilian fatalities as a counter to the stark estimates published in *The Lancet*. Certainly many groups at the time were undertaking steps to establish the numbers of deaths rather than resign themselves to Straw's apparent hopelessness. And yet, the glimpses given by FoI disclosures provide only partial pictures of what was taking place within the corridors of Whitehall, ones that can be questioned for what they conceal as well as what they reveal.

How to Look Good in a War seeks to understand the moves and machinations by states and others to depict the use of violence. The imagery of clutching shadows evokes the mindset for what follows. These are sometimes murky areas where questions of candor, secrecy, evasion, and much more besides loom large. As a result, attempting to lock in a firm grip on the facts brings its own dangers in misjudging what is within one's reach. As will be contended in later chapters, trying to understand the highly politicized issues of this book requires questioning many of the conventional assumptions and preoccupations that delimit media coverage, legal opinions, political commentary, and academic analysis.

However, more than setting out a history, *How to Look Good in a War* offers strategies for intervention. In doing so, it seeks a forward-looking agenda for scholarship and action, one that calls for rethinking the intersection of politics, law, campaigning, and technical analysis. In particular, I want to consider how moving from the typical preoccupations with establishing facts and attributing blame could usefully give way to meditating on how facts are established and how blame is attributed in the first place. That is, I want to attend to how we know what we know in order to provide new possibilities. Alternative approaches for handling evidence, uncertainty, absences, and the onus for proof will be advanced in order to hold states to account for their use of force.

IN THE MIX: KNOWLEDGE, IGNORANCE, DISCLOSURE, AND CONCEALMENT

Although evocative, the imagery of shadows brings its own dangers. The division suggested between light and dark can lend itself to simplistic and polarized thinking. It is all too easy to treat knowledge and ignorance as opposites, as with disclosure and concealment. Once pitted in this way, moral evaluations readily follow on. Other things being equal, knowledge is generally preferred to ignorance in modern times. While there might be contrasting judgments about what counts as appropriate disclosure by governments in matters of national security, the terms of the debate are typically cast in the language of needing to strike the right balance between openness and closure.

As will be argued throughout this book, such a way of thinking is highly restrictive. It closes off insights and imagination. Instead of pitching knowledge–ignorance and disclosure–concealment as opposites, it is necessary to ask how they are interrelated: the distinction between the two can blur, one can serve as a precondition for the other, and they give rise to each other.

Take knowledge and ignorance, for instance:

- The production of new facts often identifies new uncertainties and unknowns.[4]
- Assertions of unawareness amount to some claiming to be conscious of what others are not.[5]
- The decision to find out about some things can result in forgoing different possibilities. That, in turn, leads to the creation of blind spots in our understanding.[6] In this respect, each way of understanding the world 'is a sort of searchlight elucidating some of the facts and retreating the remainder into an omitted background'.[7]
- As some people come to be in the know, this has implications for the relative knowledge of everyone else.
- Some of the most valued forms of knowledge consist of appreciating the limits of what is understood.[8]

Once this fluid intermixing of knowledge and ignorance is recognized, straightforward evaluations are difficult to sustain. Ignorance need not be treated as deficiency; rather it can be seen as a conjoined twin to, an inevitable product of, and a reason for, the search for knowledge.

Likewise, concealment and disclosure are not simply opposites. Every revelation has its end. Disclosures are always partial. Without limiting what is said and placing into the background certain considerations, communication itself would be impossible.[9] Just what counts as 'concealment' versus 'disclosure' is relative. Across nations, for instance, the release of the same information by government officials might be varyingly interpreted as openness or closure. What counts as concealment or disclosure is often relational too, as what is made present shapes determinations of what is absent. As the meaning of what remains unsaid often must be interpreted from what is said, so too does the meaning of what is said get interpreted in relation to what is not. To add another twist, disclosure can work to conceal if it functions to mask what is not disclosed.

Recognition of the interrelation of knowledge and ignorance as well as disclosure and concealment is particularly important regarding matters at the center of this book: deaths to non-combatants, assessments of security threats, debates about the appropriateness of weaponry. Rather than being characterized by data vacuums or surpluses, these topics are notable for the circulation of fragmentary information wherein attention to what is missing is often evident. Especially with the emphasis attached to 'open government' in modern times, officials often shift between circulating and retaining information. Yet the very language used to describe the human cost of conflict – terms such as 'collateral damage' – is regularly questioned regarding how it obscures (and for many intentionally obscures[10]) suffering. It is within this overall complex mix that the accountability of states must be redressed.

SECRECY AND TRANSPARENCY

When knowledge–ignorance and disclosure–concealment are treated in a fluid manner, then it is possible to rethink terms like secrecy and transparency.

Secrecy

Secrecy is perhaps most often defined as intentional concealment.[11] Secret keeping then is a matter of *blocking* access and communication – achieving the opposite of disclosure.[12] The image of a water tap being turned off suggests what is entailed. The history of war is replete with attempts to hide. With varying success, the formula for Greek fire in the sixth century BC, maps of the 'New World' in the sixteenth century, and the design of atomic and nuclear weapons in the twentieth century were all subject to fierce efforts at suppression.[13] In past decades, governments in countries such as the UK have been noted for their comparative impenetrability to outside scrutiny, particularly in relation to its intelligence and military agencies.[14] 'Secrecy about secrecy' has characterized the British way.[15]

When secrecy is taken as the opposite of revelation, then those considering what information should be released are faced with a predictable – if often difficult – question: What is the right balance between openness and closure, secrecy and release?[16] The public's right to know and the state's need to restrict are set against each other. In the years that followed 9/11 many countries (most notably the US) witnessed decisive shifts in the judgment of where the proper balance rests.[17]

Even thinking of secret keeping as blocking though, not everything is as straightforward as it might appear. Openness can be a way to enhance secrecy. Soviet censors were not only schooled in taking away information, but also at using its selective release as a means of distraction and disguise.[18] They were, or are, hardly alone in this respect.[19] In matters of statecraft, the 'truthful, well-weighed answer that tells the blacker lie' has a long history.[20] Making sense of what is said and what is not is always bound up with beliefs about how to decode and what needs decoding in the first place.

By way of further developing a sense of what secret keeping entails, its *transformative* dimensions need to be acknowledged too. It is bound up with the creation of individual identities and organizational relations.[21] Entrusting some with information is to undertake a process of exclusion and inclusion. Those sharing in the secret are set apart from others as being particularly worthy, capable, etc.[22] If the unexposed learn of their exclusion, the distinction is sharpened.[23] Secrecy in this sense both indexes authority and provides a basis for it.

However, because hiding can be countered by telling, selling, stealing, and leaking, those who rely on the possession of secrets to enhance their reputation typically need to replenish ones lost.[24] It is little wonder that state agencies often try to limit access to what might otherwise be regarded as the trivial or the mundane.[25] The potential for secret keeping to set some apart is not simply determined by the content of what is restricted, but rather on the expectations surrounding what it means to be 'in the know'.

But more than this, those deemed in-group can establish what should count as a secret in the first place. As Balmer notes, operating away from public scrutiny has enabled government officials to classify, reclassify, and re-reclassify information by giving shifting arguments about who the enemy is, what they are deemed capable of, and how information is of use to them.[26]

The transformative aspects of secret keeping are also evident in the way it is part of producing cultures, identities, and ethics. A theme of the study of military research establishments is that they often operate with 'weapons cultures' that distinguish them from those of similar civilian establishments.[27] Contrary to standard thinking, secrecy can act as a useful management technique in such settings by channeling ideas.[28] It is also part of the dynamic shaping the 'moral economies' of organizations for how weapons-related research is justified.[29] Thus, assessing the appropriateness of secret keeping is inevitability bound up with judgments about the very rationales for such organizations.

Taking the rethinking of secrecy to its extreme, secrecy can be a means of *exposure*. Although somewhat counter-intuitive, this directs our attention to how the relevance of something hidden often derives from 1) that hiding being known and 2) what was once hidden becoming known.[30] So, while it is difficult to imagine something that is absolutely concealed, it is also difficult to see what relevance it could have in political life. That which is completely unknown is socially sterile.[31] Secrets are not empty spaces, but achievements negotiated over time. It is necessary therefore to consider what is shared how, among whom, and why through secrecy – this rather than just what is restricted, how, from whom, and why.

Along these lines, it is possible to note that even in relation to matters of national security, secrets can 'announce their own existence'.[32] This is so because concealing leaves traces. Maintaining total secrecy requires keeping secrets secret, and sometimes the secret of secrets secret. This is not only taxing, but also often unwanted since state officials regularly use the appeal to the privy to bolster their legitimacy and diminish that of others.[33]

Such 'open secrets' (where it is appreciated that something is deliberately withheld, but not what) contrast with 'public secrets'. The latter can refer to the elephant in the room – 'secrets' that are widely known but rarely overtly commented upon. Memories of rape in war, for instance, can be both widely acknowledged but never mentioned.[34] It is this dual quality of being present and absent, as well as remembered but unspoken, which makes it so difficult for survivors to come to terms with their past.

Transparency

If secrecy factors into knowledge–ignorance and disclosure–concealment in complex ways, then the same can be said of what it is often contrasted with: transparency.[35] Today, Open Government is typically treated as a sign of good government.[36] Making the inter-working of the state clearly visible is taken to reduce inefficiencies, nepotism, and corruption. 'Regulation by revelation' ensures accountability.[37] As with secrecy, officials can cite efforts towards openness in the pursuit of legitimacy.

However, as with secrecy, not everything is as straightforward as it might first appear. What is touted as serving democratic control –

for instance, the introduction of FoI procedures – can be said to give only the appearance of transparency.[38] The limits of what is made clear distinguish the genuine from the illusionary. The failure to achieve transparency need not simply result from a lack of openness though. If useful information is not made available in a manner that enables people to understand it, then openness can be irrelevant or even counterproductive.[39]

Following this logic further, efforts at transparency can result in *concealment*. Being clear – but on a restricted range of issues – can be used not only to divert attention, but also to create false understandings.[40] Arms control NGOs have been criticized, for instance, for attending to 'the risks of exports to the South rather than processes of Northern militarization', and thereby fostering a dubious openness about the arms trade.[41] 'Avalanching' individuals with immaterial information that they cannot find their way through has long been used by resource-rich organizations to disclose while remaining opaque.[42] Furthermore, when government agencies adopt transparency measures this can be accompanied by formal and informal attempts to discipline communications inside.[43] What is done in the name of transparency can easily blind.

The previous paragraph directs attention to how transparency – like secrecy – should be examined for how it is done in practice. It can be questioned regarding what is not done through what is done, as well as for how what is made clear obscures.[44] To the extent it is realized then, transparency is a negotiated accomplishment achieved through mechanisms that simultaneously produce non-disclosure and shape expectations of what counts as being transparent in the first place.[45] As Power warned, 'Giving an account is seen to be a way of avoiding an account' when that giving deters 'public curiosity and inquiry'.[46] Later chapters will suggest how frequently this charge could be leveled at the bureaucratic machinations that legitimize force.

An example of how transparency is accomplished while being avoided is given in Chapter 1. This looks at one of the most contentious aspects of the justification for the 2003 Iraq invasion: whether intelligence about Iraqi 'weapons of mass destruction' (WMD) was distorted in the build up to the war. Central within this chapter will be the principal British investigation into the government's portrayal of WMD, namely the 'Butler Inquiry'. As will be argued, both the Inquiry's report and its press and parliamentary reception were tension ridden. Within each, multiple and conflicting claims were given about what had been demonstrated through the Inquiry and what was beyond confirmation, as well as what had been put into the public domain and what was held back. However, almost no explicit recognition was given to such conflicts in political debates – instead they were preoccupied with assertions of 'spin' or 'no spin' made as part of blame games. So, despite the debate about WMD-claims raising questions regarding accuracy and distortion, how accuracy or distortion should be established in the first place was not treated as a matter of importance. Yet it was the subtle shifting between different 'hows' that defined and ultimately stifled political debate.

In short then, this Introduction has suggested that the pairs of knowledge–ignorance, disclosure–concealment, and transparency–secrecy are not opposed: they can coexist and each finds something of itself in the other. It is not simply that what appears as a frank revelation on the surface can actually mask a darker truth. In some ways, these pairings are inevitably implicated in one another. When the talk of surface, depth, appearance, reality, facade, inside, etc. is taken as referring to stark opposites, this can hinder appreciating what is taking place.

Once we commit ourselves to investigating this complexity, it follows that any evaluations made of statecraft cannot rely on simple stock equations such as: secrecy = bad, transparency = good.[47] That does not imply indifference or merely reversing common moral judgments. Instead, it calls for attending to details of particular issues and making any judgments in relation to those specifics.

Chapter 2 illustrates this in relation to aforementioned disputes about Iraqi deaths resulting from the 2003 invasion. To undermine the comparatively high estimations offered, the British government repeatedly spoke about why the number of deaths could not be known reliably. By drawing on materials obtained under the UK Freedom of Information Act, this chapter contests the (in)actions of government. I provide grounds for arguing that not only did the UK undertake little effort to gauge civilian deaths, but the officials embraced – if not deliberately manufactured – ignorance and ambiguity as a way of diverting, deflecting, or denying alarm. And yet, this chapter also considers the complications and tensions associated with knowing about ignorance, and in particular how the analysis of ignorance risks fostering it.

FURTHER TURNS

In line with the last comment, to take the claims in the previous two sections seriously means not only acknowledging their bearing for statecraft, but also for their study of statecraft. That is to say, *How to Look Good in a War* itself must be understood in terms of how its arguments are potentially implicated in the production of knowledge and ignorance, as well as entailing disclosure and concealment. There is no escape from this condition. Certainly the self-declared intent of an author is not enough.

All too often academics, policy commentators, NGOs, and others who investigate matters of security (or much else besides), depict themselves as the discoverers of the occult, rather than dabblers in its art.[48] This is as regrettable as it is pervasive. Whether it is because of what is studied, what is highlighted, what is left out, how uncertainty is handled, what background knowledge is drawn upon, or many other considerations besides, analysis cannot properly be conceived through only the positive connotations associated with the terms knowledge and disclosure.

To do so would hazard many dangers. One is the previously mentioned problem of overestimation. If there is anything that the study of organized violence demands, presumably it is a sensitivity to its limits. Chapters 1–3 recount intense efforts by politicians, journalists, activists, and others to lock onto the definitive truth about major areas of controversy associated with the Iraq War and other past conflicts. Yet, it is the contention of this book that if such efforts would have attended to how what was known was known, they could have been more fruitful. A second danger is that commentators can end up wrapping themselves in the prestige and mystique of the 'exposure' they are questioning in others.[49]

Another reason to avoid treating the telling of secrets as innocent is the danger of buying into the logic of revelation. Treating analysis as a means of unearthing requires being able to bring the hidden definitely to the surface. In practice this can prove elusive. A recurring theme of the chapters in Part I is that, while concealing is widespread, the concealed has a nasty habit of always being somewhere else. Because the power of secrets often derives from the advertising of their possession[50] – instead of the information withheld – attempts at exposure by some can instigate attempts by others to reconstitute what is secret. Pursuing this movement in the hopes of uncovering some final truth can invest would-be holders with a coherence and competence that might be unwarranted (see Chapters 1 and 2).

In this regard Chapter 3 examines how the said possession of information unavailable to outsiders worked to bolster the legitimacy of violence. It does so in relation to the use of 'cluster bombs'. Against repeatedly voiced concern, countries such as the US, Israel, and Russia maintained that the correct balance between humanity and military necessity (as required under international humanitarian law) had been struck in the use of these weapons. However, governments have steadfastly refused to detail how this balance has been made. For far too long, in pitching their opposition through the confines of international humanitarian law, critical organizations and officials set themselves up as needing to uncover and counter the calculations made by user states. Evidence is presented in this chapter that these strategies credited major user governments with a grossly misplaced regard for the humanitarian effects of their force. When reform-minded individuals shifted away from the language of the 'law' and 'balances' to one of 'patterns' and 'presumptions', we were able to make uncertainties and unknowns sources of advantage.

Instead of positioning itself as setting out some final truth, *How to Look Good in a War* asks how those concerned about organized violence can intervene so as to make a difference in how it is understood and orchestrated. The goal then is to find ways of transforming 'problematic situations'[51] through fostering actionable knowledge about both the practice of statecraft as well as the practices for intervention into it. Sensitive to its limitations, a starting premise is that our means of engagement need to be open to revision. This is so, not least, because what proves useful at one point in time can later turn sterile. Rather than setting out definitive histories and grounds for opposition, this book seeks to cultivate mindsets and orientations.

What the anthropologist Michael Taussig called 'the craving for certainty that secrecy inspires'[52] is also addressed in *How to Look Good in a War* by experimenting with non-conventional forms of writing. Chapter 4 offers a conversational account between the author and prominent activists regarding how cluster bombs become subject to a major international ban. Tensions, uncertainties, and contradictions associated with knowing and conveying matters that cannot be wholly known or conveyed are worked through. One goal of the overt play between knowledge and ignorance in this chapter is to sensitize readers to how secrets, unknowns, and absences figure within the practices of statecraft, attempts to alter them, and later accounts of both. A second is to encourage the kind of deft mindfulness that befits the investigation of the topics of this book.

Part II builds on the experiences and lessons presented in Part I in order to identify possibilities for the future. Chapter 5 does so by outlining more generic strategies that can be pursued by progressive campaigners, officials, academics, and others. The role of evidence and facts, precaution, stigmatization, international law, and the politics of consistency are among the topics addressed. These will be looked to not so much as bases for settling disputes but rather as sites of possibility. As elsewhere in the book, attention to limits – in what can be known and what can be expressed – will be looked to for inspiration. Avenues for reflection and intervention are sought, that lead to the generation of new possibilities – ones that can then suggest paths for subsequent cycles of reflection and intervention.

On the back of the first five chapters, Chapter 6 examines one area for future political mobilization: the use of explosive weapons. Among other recent conflicts, their use was central to the justifications for and criticism of the 2011 NATO intervention in Libya. Just as cluster bombs eventually became seen as a category of weaponry in need of major international scrutiny, this chapter asks how the emerging recognition of the category of 'explosive weapons' could provide a basis for reducing the humanitarian consequences of armed violence. Alternative possibilities are contrasted to show how the debate about this class of weaponry could be framed in the future. Framing here refers to the organizing principles used for understanding the world – how problems are diagnosed, causes identified, and solutions recommended. In doing so, this chapter proposes the choices and tensions that concerned NGOs, government officials, journalists, and others face in establishing and addressing a topic of concern. Paths are sought for initiating a process of categorization and framing that reduces the harms of armed violence while also questioning how those harms are conceived. The final chapter presents some concluding thoughts.

Part I
Partial Revelations

1
Show and Tell: Distortion, Concealment, and WMD

The Introduction proposed that understanding how violence is depicted and defended requires the reconsideration of many common ways of thinking. For instance, concealment–disclosure and transparency–secrecy are not simply opposites. Instead they can coexist, fade into each other, and stem from each other. As a consequence, strives for greater openness can obscure as they divulge.

This chapter takes these initial points further. It does so in relation to one of the most contentious aspects of the 2003 Iraq invasion: claims made about 'weapons of mass destruction' (WMD). In the words of the former British Prime Minster Tony Blair, assessments of Iraqi WMD were part of the justification for why the threat from Saddam Hussein's regime was 'serious and current' and why he had 'to be stopped'.[1] The failure after the invasion to find such weapons led to numerous recriminations against those governments that pressed for intervention.

This chapter charts how the restriction *and* the release of information associated with government portrayals of intelligence weaved together into a blindfold. The aim is not to voice yet another opinion about whether intelligence had really been 'spun', but to map the logic that defined and delimited political debate about spinning.

This is done by meditating on the question: 'What is before us?'. So much of the controversy about the representation of intelligence centered on what was in clear sight: the language of government statements. Yet, in many respects, the political disputes that played out neglected language. By considering how attention was and was not given to wording, it will be possible to consider the basis for the legitimacy.

Within the overall argument of this book, a purpose of this chapter is to illustrate the mental dexterity needed to delve into the practices of statecraft. It will set the basis for proactive interventions in later chapters.

LEGITIMACY AND PUBLICITY

A history of the role of intelligence in the Iraq invasion cannot be told without reference to *hiding*. The military campaign that began on March 20, 2003 had its origins in the intrigue of past Iraqi attempts to deny, disguise, and deceive – particularly in relation to its nuclear, chemical, and biological programs. Both before and after the 1991 Gulf War, governments and international observers underestimated or otherwise badly misjudged such capabilities. In the build up to the 2003 invasion, the specter was raised of an Iraq in possession of what were deemed 'weapons of mass destruction'.[2] That the inspectors sent into Iraq in 2002 under a UN Security Council Resolution failed to find such weapons simply hardened the pre-war views of some that meticulous concealment was afoot.[3]

A history of the role of intelligence in the invasion also cannot be told without reference to *revelation*. Leading politicians in the nations that would compose the multinational military force repeatedly sought to out Iraqi attempts to obtain WMD. In the autumn of 2002, for instance, the British government and the Central Intelligence Agency (CIA) published unclassified documents setting out what they knew about Iraq's WMD.[4] Perhaps the most viewed instance of intelligence-made-public was the UN Security Council address by US Secretary of State Colin Powell on February 5, 2003. Powell put on global display communication intercepts, satellite images, and detainee statements that normally would have stayed tightly controlled.

Further, a history of the Iraq invasion cannot be told without reference to the contorted relation between revelation and hiding. As Gusterson noted, while Powell appeared to put novel information on the table for all, his presentation was full of rhetorical sleights that suggested things were not necessarily as they might appear.[5] Satellite imaginary of alleged chemical munitions bunkers, for instance, were said to be 'sometimes hard for the average person to interpret, hard for me. The painstaking work of photo analysis takes experts with years and years of experience, poring for hours and hours over light tables'.[6] Thus, although the photos were presented for all to see, their meaning had been deciphered by trained (American) specialists.[7]

Attention to the 'not-as-it-would-seem' relation between the sender–message–receiver was evident elsewhere. For some, what was shown was *not* what was vital. So, the relatively poor quality of the evidence presented at the UN was taken as heightening the expectation of what the US really knew. This was so since it was assumed that the US would withhold its best material so as not to divulge its true surveillance capabilities.[8]

With the failure to find WMD, the smooth confidences that characterized pre-invasion claims by politicians in the US, the UK, Australia, the Netherlands[9] and elsewhere gradually gave way to stuttering defenses. One by one the major planks of the Iraqi WMD threat came under scrutiny through public reviews and media investigations.[10] Plain facts – about mobile laboratories for biological weapons or Iraq's attempts to acquire high-strength aluminum tubes for its nuclear program – were declared as wanting. With this, the public face of pre-war government unanimity gave way to a picture of discord and infighting – as in the relation between the US Vice President's Office, the CIA, and the State Department.[11] The suppression of contradictory evidence, planted news stories, and false human intelligence obtained under torture were cited to ask whether those who evoked the WMD threat – such as Colin Powell – were deceived by others, whether they deceived others, or whether they deceived themselves (again[12]).[13]

Predictably with the finger pointing that ensued, the relation between what intelligence agencies concluded and what political leaders stated became a locus for attention. Questions were asked regarding whether intelligence was being fixed around policy and whether public presentations acted to mask uncertainties.

This chapter focuses on these concerns about the accuracy of intelligence claims. It does so for the UK. Here, perhaps more than in any other country, concerns about the threats and legality of WMD were central to the government's case for war.

INTELLIGENCE HISTORIES

A history of the role of British intelligence in the Iraq invasion should not be told without acknowledging the disagreement evident about what should be included within any such history.

For instance, the previous section noted the production in September 2002 of a document entitled *Iraq's Weapons of Mass Destruction – The Assessment of the British Government* (commonly known as the 'September Dossier'). The Prime Minister stated this dossier was 'based, in large part, on the work of the Joint Intelligence Committee [JIC]'.[14] The JIC sits at the hub of the intelligence agencies. It is mainly composed of the heads of intelligence services. Until the September Dossier, it had never produced a public document or had its assessments explicitly drawn on as part of a call to action.[15]

And yet, while the September Dossier was the official public face of intelligence, its importance has been contrastingly presented as part of alternative accounts of whether culpability needed to be leveled. Some commentators and the Butler Inquiry (see below), downplayed the role of the dossier in persuading the public and, by implication, diminished the gravity of any wording discrepancy.[16] Others made the opposite argument to support alternative conclusions.

One of those was the former British Broadcasting Corporation (BBC) reporter Andrew Gilligan. During a 6.07am *Today Programme* news report on May 29, 2003, he claimed that a senior official involved in the drafting of the September Dossier had told him that the Prime Minister's Office 'ordered a week before publication, ordered it to be sexed up, to be made more exciting and ordered more facts to be er, to be discovered'.[17] With regard to the claim in the September Dossier that intelligence supported the judgment that some Iraqi WMD would be deployable within 45 minutes of an order to use them,[18] at the 6:07am broadcast Gilligan said that 'the government probably erm, knew that that forty five minute figure was wrong, even before it decided to put it in'.[19] Whether or not it mattered that he did not use (or correct) this wording in subsequent BBC broadcasts that day was one of the many issues that would later divide commentators.

During 2003, both the House of Commons Intelligence and Security Committee and its Foreign Affairs Committee considered pre-war intelligence claims, though with curtailed information-gathering powers.[20] While raising some points of criticism, (notably about the '45 minutes claim'), neither concluded anything close to the government having 'sexed up' or politicized intelligence. Had it not been for a tragic event, these reports would have likely stood as official political history.

Prior to testifying before the House of Commons Committees in early July 2003, Dr. David Kelly was identified by the Ministry of Defence as the senior official referred to by Andrew Gilligan. On July 18 he was found dead. The Prime Minister initiated an inquiry chaired by Lord Hutton to investigate this death. As part of concluding that David Kelly had committed suicide, the Hutton Inquiry also dismissed allegations that the government had knowingly embellished intelligence. The lack of scrutiny given to how the September Dossier was sourced, drafted, and presented was part of why many branded the Hutton Inquiry's report a 'whitewash' favoring the government[21] – although others again downplayed concerns, including those regarding the influence by the Prime Minister's Office on the Dossier's drafting.[22]

Noting the importance attached to wording nuances is also a way to signal the dimensions of dispute. Whether or not intelligence had been distorted turned on what Dr. David Kelly called 'word-smithing' – the details of what gets said and how it is expressed.[23] The subtle use of language could disguise uncertainties and bolster fragile hunches. So as part of the Hutton Inquiry it was asked: Was it acceptable to include the language 'As a result of the intelligence we judge' with regard to the 45-minute statement? Or would an appropriate wording have been 'intelligence indicates'?[24]

In such disputes, it is difficult to imagine that any simple and universal metric could have sufficed to establish faithfulness and correctness. Then, as now, arguments about what is important and why, regarding what gets said, are perhaps better thought of as leading to assessments of similarity; this rather than a similarity deriving from some underlining essence of what makes some words sufficiently like others.[25] Any text is always open to multiple readings and reinterpretations depending on what is seen as germane for understanding it.

Complicating the situation further, central allegations of the distortion dispute – such as 'sexed up' or 'WMD' – were themselves clearly open to interpretation. Professor Diane Coole argued that the Hutton Report was able to be labeled a whitewash because it treated 'sexing up' in black and white terms: 'Had the government knowingly lied?' versus 'Had it made the strongest claims permitted?'. This treatment had the effect of eliminating 'by fiat a grey area where words, meanings and representations remain ambiguous and open to a variety of interpretations, such that the distinctions between representation, presentation and misrepresentation defy definitive judgements of truth versus falsity.'[26]

After a parallel statement in the US, on February 3, 2004 the British Prime Minister announced a wide-ranging inquiry into intelligence on weapons of mass destruction, including 'any discrepancies between the intelligence gathered, evaluated and used by the Government' in relation to pre-war Iraqi WMD.[27] The appointed five-member committee was chaired by Lord Butler. Unlike the previously mentioned investigations in the UK, each of which worked under major limitations in terms of their access to information powers,[28] the inquiry team read intelligence reports and other confidential materials.

What become known as the 'Butler Inquiry' would assume a high visibility in UK politics. In an effort to establish facts and learn lessons, its work was located at the center of political dispute about the rights and wrongs of the Iraq war. As suggested by the previous argument in this chapter, its attempts to determine whether politicized distortion had taken place were about spin, open to charges as having been delivered as spin, and able to be spun by others.

On the last point, the question of just what the Butler Inquiry had actually concluded would figure prominently in coverage of its publication. Certain collective government failures were identified, but it did not single out politicians, their advisors, or members of the intelligence community for personal reprimand.[29] No evidence was presented for 'deliberate distortion' or 'culpable negligence' of the assessment of intelligence. Ministers and advisors were not judged to have politically interfered with the production of the September Dossier. As in the US, when blame was identified it was largely directed at intelligence agencies.[30] The report identified certain areas of criticism for the JIC, such as the lack of qualifications about the basis for intelligence or the 45-minute claim.

Yet, as opposed to the Hutton Inquiry, the Butler Inquiry was not widely labeled as a whitewash. So how did the inquiry make the case for the overall legitimacy of government portrayals of intelligence? How did detractors of the war try to counter this evaluation? And how, as part of advancing these cases, did commentators make a case for the legitimacy of their own interpretations about distortion?

The answer is, in many different ways. And it was the advancing of these alternatives that carved the bounds of political debate: limits that were clearly visibly, but also rendered unseen.

'SEXED UP' INTELLIGENCE?

By way of sketching the twists and turns of what was said, this section considers the following, in relation to the arguments forwarded regarding whether intelligence had been sexed up and how this evaluation was justified:

- The Butler Report published on July 14, 2004;
- References to it in major British national newspapers[31] and the UK parliament[32] in the six months that followed its publication;[33]

- Testimony by Lord Butler to the House of Commons Select Committee on Public Administration on October 21, 2004. As part of an investigation into the effectiveness of public inquiries, this committee of members of parliament (MPs) was able to question witnesses at length.

Obviously Not Spun

To turn to the Butler Report itself, of note here is that the said faithfulness of the wording in the September Dossier was demonstrated – not by a detailed analysis of the meaning and significance of words – but rather by restating (some of) the very language disputed.

So the chapters in the report dealing with Iraqi intelligence included a section titled 'The Accuracy of the Dossier'. Its five pages consisted of four tables addressing Iraqi regime intent, chemical and biological agents, delivery systems, and nuclear weapons, with brief pre- and post-table commentaries.[34] The tables set quotes from JIC assessments and the September Dossier side-by-side.

Extract 1.1 reproduces the table dealing with Iraqi delivery systems. The conclusion offered in paragraph 339 was that the JIC judgments were 'reflected fairly' in the September Dossier. By representing certain wording, 'The Accuracy of the Dossier' section treats establishing distortion as straightforward. Besides the short commentary after the table, resemblance is taken as obvious and established. No special expertise or access to information is required to make sense of the columns. What is called 'accuracy' here is taken to be a matter of the likeness of words which can be found by direct examination of the words themselves.

Obviously Spun

Given that the column comparisons were the central means in the Butler Report for demonstrating the faithfulness of the September Dossier, a peculiar feature of the newspaper and parliamentary commentary was the almost complete absence of attention to the tables. Only three brief references were made to the column comparison method in the British newspapers examined and two in parliament.[35]

Perhaps even more peculiar, each asserted evaluations to the effect that the tables clearly demonstrated how the dossier was *at*

Extract 1.1: Faithfulness in Columns

THE ACCURACY OF THE DOSSIER

333. In general, subject to the points below and others identified in Chapter 6, the statements in the dossier reflected fairly the judgements of past JIC assessments. In the tables in the paragraphs below, quotations from JIC assessments are set out in the left-hand column and from the dossier are set out in the right-hand column.

(...)

338. Delivery systems:

Quotations from JIC Assessments	Quotations from the dossier
Iraq told UNSCOM in the 1990s that it filled 25 warheads with anthrax, botulinum toxin and aflatoxin for its Al Hussein ballistic missile (range 650km). Iraq also admitted it had developed 50 chemical warheads for Al Hussein. We judge Iraq retains up to 20 Al Husseins and a limited number of launchers. [9 September]	*Iraq told UNSCOM that it filled 25 warheads with anthrax, botulinum toxin and aflatoxin. Iraq also developed chemical agent warheads for al-Hussein. Iraq admitted to producing 50 chemical warheads for al-Hussein which were intended for the delivery of a mixture of sarin and cyclosarin.* [Chapter 3, paragraph 14]
Iraq is also developing short-range systems Al Samoud/Ababil 100 ballistic missiles (range 150kms plus) – One intelligence report suggests that Iraq has "lost" the capability to develop warheads capable of effectively disseminating chemical and biological agent and that it would take six months to overcome the "technical difficulties". However, both these missiles systems are currently being deployed with military units and an emergency operational capability with conventional warheads is probably available. [9 September]	*Al-Samoud/Ababil 100 ballistic missiles (range 150kms plus): it is unclear if chemical and biological warheads have been developed for these systems, but given the Iraqi experience on other missile systems, we judge that Iraq has the technical expertise for doing so.* [Chapter 3, paragraph 14] [The dossier] *discloses that his military planning allows for some of the WMD to be ready within 45 minutes of an order to use them.* [Prime Minister's Foreword] *Iraq has: ... military plans for the use of chemical and biological weapons, including against its own Shia population. Some of these weapons are deployable within 45 minutes of an order to use them.* [Executive Summary, paragraph 6]
Iraq has probably dispersed its special weapons, including its CBW weapons. Intelligence also indicates that chemical and biological munitions could be with military units and ready for firing within 20–45 minutes. [9 September]	*Iraq's military forces are able to use chemical and biological weapons, with command, control and logistical arrangements in place. The Iraqi military are able to deploy these weapons within 45 minutes of a decision to do so.* [Chapter 3, paragraph 1] *... intelligence indicates that as part of Iraq's military planning Saddam is willing to use chemical and biological weapons, including against his own Shia population. Intelligence indicates that the Iraqi military are able to deploy chemical or biological weapons within 45 minutes of an order to do so.* [Chapter 3, paragraph 5]

339. JIC judgements on Iraq's ballistic missile capabilities were reflected fairly in the dossier. The '45 minute' issue was, because of the context of the JIC assessment, run together in the dossier with statements on Iraqi intentions for use of its capabilities. It was also included in the Prime Minister's Foreword.

odds with the JIC assessments. For instance, the former government intelligence analyst Crispin Black argued that Lord Butler:

> would not dream of using the demotic 'sexed up', but the way the evidence is presented allows us to draw our own conclusions. By publishing excerpts of the original joint intelligence committee papers and placing them alongside the dodgy dossier, he and his colleagues demonstrate the great gulf in words and tone and intended meaning between the real JIC assessments and the September Dossier.[36]

To those commentators who said the tables indicated that the JIC assessments were at odds with the September Dossier, it did not seem to matter that the readings were themselves at odds with the Butler Inquiry's 'fair reflection' judgment given in paragraph 333. What they shared with the Inquiry was the latter's suggestion in 'The Accuracy of the Dossier' section that no special knowledge was required to make determinations of faithfulness – the answer could simply be found by looking at the words.

Obviously Spun (Once Decoded)

Another type of contrary reading was made widely in the press and parliament. In this case, meaning retreated from the page to instead be found in the mind of one of those that penned it.

Particularly owning to the 'Mandarin' (senior civil bureaucrat) background of Lord Butler, numerous suggestions were made to the effect that 'what the Butler Report states is not what the report really means'.[37,38] As one columnist put it, Lord Butler was never going to have used the language of 'screw-ups and false claims' that were given in the parallel American intelligence inquires. This was so because Butler:

> was a former cabinet secretary, an establishment insider who spent a lifetime mastering the art of the coded memo, the veiled policy paper. His report was never going to be the searing, damning indictment some had longed for. That would be far too crude.

As such, the lack of outright condemnation in the report was not sign of absolution. Indeed, the deliberate and careful language of officialdom made its critical sting 'all the more powerful'.[39] Uncovering that sting required translating Butler's 'deliberately understated' civil service-speak.[40] The newspaper *The Independent* did so by producing seven comparisons between 'What Butler says' and 'What it means', including:

> The 45-minute claim
> What Butler says: The JIC should not have concluded [sic: included] the '45-minute' report in its assessment and in the Government's dossier without stating what it was believed to refer to. The fact that the reference in the classified assessment was repeated in the dossier later led to suspicions that it had been included because of its eye-catching character.
> What it means: The 45-minute claim was added to make the case for war look better, and it was wrong to use it without making it clear that it never referred to anything more than battlefield munitions. Had it done so, of course, it would have underlined the fact that the threat to anyone outside the immediate battlefield in question was nil. That would have meant no arresting headlines, and, indeed, would have changed the whole way the nation perceived Saddam Hussein's potency.[41]

Just who was capable of decoding the report to uncover its true meaning was a matter on which different assessments were forwarded.[42,43]

Sticking to Words

The picture outlined so far only begins to chart the sorts of moves made in the discussion about sexing up. At least in certain respects, and at certain times, attention was given to precise wording. During his testimony questioning before the Select Committee on Public Administration, Lord Butler queried the differences between the report's text and how committee members summarized it.[44] For example, to the Chairman's proposal that the Butler Report was 'pretty devastating' (and much else besides) for the way the UK was governed, Butler countered:

> You may say that the report is expressed in Mandarin but these are, if I may say so, pretty dramatic terms which we did not use. We did not use phrases like 'bolts of lightning' or 'devastating' or anything like that. What we did say – and I think I would rather like to stick to the words – is 'We do not suggest that there is or should be an ideal or unchangeable system of collective government. Still less, that procedures are in aggregate any less effective now than in earlier times.' [...] That is what we said.

People can draw their own conclusions from it and you are but we did not express ourselves in quite the dramatic terms which are being represented here.[45]

In contrast to the column in Extract 1.1, here Butler attends to the differences between the words in the report and the words of the Chairman. While some scope was made for people to draw their own conclusions, that latitude did not extend to the Chairman's said dramatic representations.

Deferred Judgment

Going back the Butler Report itself, any clear-cut suggestion about how its table columns demonstrated its 'fair reflection' conclusions is complicated by the fact that in other places that resemblance is not presented as self-evident. In the section immediately prior to 'The Accuracy of the Dossier', the column comparison approach was also used to put JIC assessment and dossier claims about the size and quality of the intelligence basis side-by-side. The introduction to that table stated:

> 329. In this Section we examine the way in which judgements in JIC assessments prepared during 2002 were translated into the dossier. We are acutely aware of the danger of being unfair through selective quotation. The dossier did not follow the format of JIC assessments exactly, nor should it have done so. It was written for a different purpose and a different audience. Furthermore, to be comprehensive it brought together the key parts of a number of past JIC assessments, together with some intelligence that had not featured in JIC assessments, about Iraq's nuclear, biological, chemical and ballistic missile programmes. It is as a result difficult to make a direct comparison between judgements in any one JIC paper and the language in the dossier. We are therefore publishing, at Annex B, substantial extracts from three key JIC assessments issued in 2002 alongside relevant extracts from the Government's dossier, the Prime Minister's Foreword and his accompanying statement to the House of Commons so that readers can check our judgements and reach their own conclusions.[46]

In this passage, the problems of selective quotation were compounded by those of direct likening. In recognition of the purpose and audience of communication, Annex B gave further column comparisons so that 'readers can check our judgements and reach their own conclusions'.

However, the relation between Annex B, 'The Intelligence behind the Dossier' section, and 'The Accuracy of the Dossier' section is not certain. Paragraph 329 does not make explicit reference to the table comparisons offered in the 'The Accuracy of the Dossier' section. Yet, since that section immediately followed, it used the same column comparison. Annex B was also relevant to concerns about accuracy, and the qualifications in paragraph 329 seem to relate to the tables in Extract 1.1.

The idea that the topics addressed by the Butler Inquiry were matters on which individuals could make their own judgments was echoed in Butler's testimony before the Select Committee on Public Administration.[47] For instance, its Chairman asked why the Butler Report did not make reference to a conclusion in the JIC's February 2003 assessment. The House of Commons Intelligence and Security Committee (ISC) – which has unique parliamentary access to intelligence documents – chose to publicize in one of its reports that a 2003 JIC assessment concluded that: 'any collapse of the Iraqi regime would increase the risk of chemical and biological warfare, technology or agents finding their way into the hands of terrorists, not necessarily al-Qaeda'.[48]

At issue here then was not what the Butler Report *included*, but what it *excluded*. Those things left out that never made it into 'The Accuracy of the Dossier' section or anywhere in the report. Butler responded that while the Chairman might have found it worth referring to, 'The ISC report had already been published. We did not feel it necessary to go over everything that the ISC had disclosed. You may say we should have criticized the Government on that ground, but we did not, we saw the document'. Thus here as in paragraph 329 of the report, Butler both acknowledges the scope for alterative judgments while also advancing his own evaluation. That this judgment was based on evaluating documents not available to most parliamentarians, let alone the general public, meant his reasoning was obscured.

Being Told

And yet, the scope for others to make their own judgments was seemingly curtailed elsewhere. Diligent readers that followed the prompt in paragraph 329 to Annex B would have read at the bottom of each page the qualification: 'Redactions are not indicated'. So while individuals could reach their own conclusions, they would have to do so without all the information. Since this redaction qualification did not suggest what had been removed, readers would also have to reach conclusions without information about what information was missing. However, in practice this seems to have been taken for little. None of the five newspaper and parliamentary commentators that contended the tables clearly demonstrated how the dossier was at odds with the JIC assessments noted this redaction limitation or suggested it might compromise their ability to offer evaluations of spin.

Elsewhere, more direct suggestions were made that readers of the Butler Report were reliant on trusting the judgment of select others. As part of the critical questioning in the Select Committee on Public Administration about parliament getting access to evidence that could determine the truthfulness of intelligence claims, Butler retorted that:

> You know what happened. Our report tells you what happened. What it tells you is that there were intelligence reports, some of which since the war have turned out to be unreliable. You have been told that. [...] You have also been told that the Joint Intelligence Committee reached conclusions on the basis of the intelligence they had which were truthfully reported in public, but that in our view, you should also have been told that the intelligence underlying them was thin. You have been told all that. There is nothing more to tell you. As Privy Councillors,[49] we were able to look into the details of intelligence which, for perfectly good and important reasons, cannot be made public. We have to be trusted on that. If you do not trust us on that, that machinery has failed, but I think you can trust us on it.[50]

In contrast to paragraph 329 of the Butler Report, no scope is given in this statement to the possibility for alternative judgments in this part of the testimony. In contrast to 'The Accuracy of the Dossier' section of the report that treated faithfulness as being shown through the tables, the contention here is that the Butler Report *told* the evaluation of an expert inquiry set apart from others by its access to otherwise inaccessible details. The Select Committee MPs were not informed about the content of such secrets, but merely that there were secrets.

In a curious way then, when pressed under testimony, Butler ends where his inquiry began: it was invested with a trusted authority to scrutinize whether intelligence had been manipulated and its ultimate conclusions were defended from criticism by contending that the reading made of secret intelligence had to be trusted.[51] Not only did the existence of this inaccessible intelligence imply Butler and his inquiry members should be given a high status, by implication it simultaneously lowered the importance of what previously had been in public circulation.[52]

LANGUAGE AND OPENNESS

The September Dossier was portrayed as unprecedented in the UK for its public presentation of intelligence.[53] As an official investigation into discrepancies of how the government represented intelligence, the Butler Report was in its own way unprecedented.

Making sense of the real meaning of intelligence is often said to be riddled with pitfalls. The previous section suggested much the same could be said about making sense of the review of the use of intelligence. By going beyond the preoccupations in headline reporting about whether intelligence was really 'sexed-up', a purpose was to outline the shifting arguments made about both whether intelligence had been distorted and – crucially – how this could be determined.

If the questions are asked 'How open (or secretive) was the British government about what it knew regarding Iraqi WMD threat?' or 'How open (or secretive) was the Butler Inquiry about what it knew about what the British government knew?' then a definitive answer seems misplaced. Meaning was made present and allusive. What was said to be a transparent setting-out of evidence in one situation was elsewhere said to require restricted knowledge to understand properly.

Yet, critically, this positioning was not itself a topic of attention either in the official review of government claims or the scrutiny of that review by prominent political commentators.[54] This should lead to caution in the conclusions drawn. For instance, against her previously mentioned criticisms of the Hutton Report relying on a black-and-white distinction of 'sexing up', Diane Coole positively contrasted the Butler Report to it. This was justified, not because the latter

> reversed Hutton's conclusions but because of its willingness to enter that crucial zone of ambiguity that I am accusing Hutton of vacating. Although aspects of [the Butler Report], were criticized, it courted nothing like the controversy of its predecessor. Might

this not in part be because its underlying assumptions are more congruent with its purpose?[55]

Yet this chapter has cast doubt on any single characterization of underlying assumptions. The report, and Butler's later presentation of it, entered and existed in zones of ambiguity – both about how it interpreted the September Dossier and how to interpret the Butler Inquiry's examination of it. Rather than saying that the report did not court controversy because of its underlying assumptions, it seems closer to the mark to say that it did not court controversy because of the numerous underlying assumptions associated with it. Beyond the Butler Report itself, parliamentarians, reporters, and political pundits likewise gave contrasting emphasis to interpretation.

Notable as part of the overall debate was the lack of attention to the shifting arguments about how determinations of distortion should be established. Sometimes different words were treated as the same, sometimes as consequently dissimilar. Sometimes words were decoded for their hidden meaning, sometimes they were taken as having a face-value meaning. Sometimes words were given meaning, sometimes words were said to require meaning to be given to them.

In consequential ways then, the debate about the report's findings regarding faithfulness reads as an assortment of claims jumbled together. While criticism was leveled (or not) and blame assigned (or not), the basis for these evaluations was generally not part of the discussion. Often definitive assertions regarding the manipulation were advanced while leaving untouched how they were supported, how they conflicted with other assessments, or the limitations of the knowledge that supported them. As a result, whatever unstated data and inferences individuals drew on were not aired.

If transparency is not just a matter of what gets said but how information is made sense of in practice, then the degree of openness achieved through the debate that followed the Butler Report is doubtful. A shared failure to examine collective terms of debate would seem an apt summation. An albeit polite (typically, anyway) shouting match would be another. As a result of the preoccupations of the debate, evaluations of political distortion were sealed from detailed scrutiny and from a perceived need for scrutiny.

This overall condition – one in which arguments about likeness were being forwarded without shared attention to how this was being done – created the circumstances in which evaluations and counter-evaluations of distortion could endlessly be reopened. So in the years that followed the publication of the Butler Report, the release of previously inaccessible evidence was accompanied by running claims about how this latest evidence brought into the light proved (or proved once decoded/proved to those in the know) whether or not intelligence had been spun.[56] Yet again, this was done without attention to the basis for determinations of likeness.

In the bounded terms of the political debate, one idea that did not receive much attention in the press or parliament was the limitation of expertise. So the contention that determinations of politicization were simply too subtle, and were too bound to contextually derived meaning, were open to multiple interpretations, were simply too unruly to be established definitively by an elite committee of overseers marked by the bounds of conventional commentary.

BETRAYING WORDS

What then does the previous analysis suggest for the central concern of this book: how attempts are made to look good in a war? In relation to the sort of expert oversight bodies represented by the Butler Inquiry, for instance, several lessons could be identified:

Lesson 1 – Above all, multiply: When tasked with offering an appraisal of a complex and contentious topic (such as determining the faithfulness of words), one strategy is to forward varied accounts of how your determinations were reached.

Lesson 2 – Make the multiplying a non-issue: That varied accounts are being offered should not itself be a matter of attention. To avoid this, some distance must be established between the accounts – whether that is in terms of a time delay or the audience listening. Besides avoiding claims of duplicity, this will allow you to 'multiply and divide'.

Lesson 3 – Multiply and divide: With many accounts in hand of how your appraisal was reached, it is possible to counter unfriendly suggestions by shifting back and forth between the many bases of determinations.

Lesson 4 – In gray you can play: Ambiguity cannot be underestimated as a resource. Clarity marks out trench lines for conflict. A lack of it leaves much scope for maneuvering. The skill is in producing shades that enables the creative drawing on a sense of context, facts, background, and so on, to move as required, to declare censuses when needed, to spark division when desired, etc.

Lesson 5 – If knowledge is power, ignorance is power: Managing the accessibility of information is a way of managing relations of expertise and accountability. Depending on the situation, both claiming knowledge and ignorance might be advantageous. Ambiguity in relation to what you know is a way of resisting lines of interrogation. Making questioners uncertain about what they know is a way of undermining questioning itself.

Lesson 6 – Allowing judged judgment: As part of producing ambiguity, acknowledging the potential for others to draw their own conclusions can be a way of ensuring that your own (official) version does not get directly challenged.

This listing is meant as an ironic summary rather than a deciphered codebook. There is no sense in which it is being claimed that the Butler Inquiry members or others intentionally acted according to these rules. As will be examined in Chapter 2, attributing underlining strategies to individuals is often part of what needs to be resisted. What the listing is meant to do is to bring to the fore certain dynamics examined above.

This chapter closes with a few reflections for those that seek to assess the basis for the legitimacy of state violence. First, it is necessary to recognize the limits of conventional political questioning. It was not so much the case that the bounds on the debate were established *despite* the extensive coverage of the politicization of intelligence, but rather *because* of it. The repeated forwarding of confident assessments of blame without considering how blame was attributed provided the conditions in which public debate could run and run (and run).

Second, following on from this point, the search for definitive understanding can hazard not only sidelining how debates unfold, but it can buy into questionable assumptions. For the topics examined in this chapter, attempts to uncover some final truth regarding what really happened would arguably invest individuals and the debate overall with a misplaced coherence.

Third, while this chapter has sought to avoid some of the hazards associated with making determinations of spin, it cannot avoid all the hazards of making evaluations. In selecting particular issues for consideration and leaving others out, in providing 'upshot' glosses of texts, in restating the terms of particular debates, in making claims of likeness, in briefly characterizing complex events, and in much else besides, this analysis is readily susceptible to the types of arguments of distortion it is meant to be analyzing. This stands not as a refutation of this analysis but confirmation of the conditions of any analysis. This suggests a continuing need to examine our own claims while examining those of officialdom.

2
Estimating Ignorance

The debate in Chapter 1 centered on a troubling condition: with the ability to communicate comes the possibility for deception as well as the possibility for making allegations of deception (that in themselves might involve subterfuge).

With the failure to find anything like functioning WMDs, the inquiries into the presentation of intelligence about Iraq acted as contests about whether publics had been mislead by their political leaders. In these investigations, concerns about how words revealed and hid dovetailed with concerns about what was being made public and what was being held back. As part of pointing out who was to blame (or not), multiple bases for assessing the likeness of words were used. This was done without attention to there being multiple bases or detailed scrutiny to the soundness of reasoning used. While this situation was lamentable, Chapter 1 ended with a point of caution about how attempts to analyze language can end up relying on the forms of argument they are questioning.

This chapter considers another major area of controversy associated with the 2003 Iraq invasion: civilian deaths. A sense of the number of deaths has underpinned many assessments of the rights and wrongs of this conflict.[1] As with the previous chapter, this one elaborates how state officials offered multiple claims about what could be known without attending to this or without attending to the soundness of the bases for the evaluations being proffered. As with the previous chapter though, in this one dangers are identified with attempts to cut through the appearance of events.

The focus is not only on how claims to concealment and disclosure mix, but also those to knowledge and ignorance. Unlike the previous chapter, this one goes a step further in asking how otherwise inaccessible information can be collected and assessed. It does so both to understand how the consequences of statecraft are defended and to set the stage for considering the possibilities for intervention.

HISTORIES OF DEATH

The killing of those not engaged in fighting has been an issue throughout the written record of conflict.[2] What can be said with some confidence about this long and checkered history is that the acceptability of non-combatant deaths has been subject to varying evaluation over time.

To take just one example, as World War II approached 'total war', civilian deaths were commonplace. The saturation bombing of major cities in Europe and the Pacific sought to inflict suffering and terror that the populaces on the ground could not endure. While regarded as more or less regrettable among operations planners, there could have been little doubt that people would die in substantial numbers as cities were reduced to smoking rubble.[3] Official estimations on the number of those killed were bound up with domestic and international politics. At times, deaths to enemy populations were inflated so as to bolster the lethality of force.[4] Particularly after fighting ceased though, concerns about whether victorious domestic populations might come to regret what had been done in their name led to a reluctance to know the effects of bombing.[5]

The legitimacy of civilians as targets has shifted as the definition of the enemy has shifted. When populations are seen as supporting the war effort – as was often the case in World War II – then deaths become more palatable. Since the end of the Cold War, high on the agenda of Western governments have been rogue and failed states. Within these, the populations cannot be blamed for the actions of their political elite. Indeed, military interventions led by the US into places such as Iraq, Yugoslavia, and Afghanistan have been justified as bringing humanitarian relief to subjugated peoples. As such, inflicting unnecessary civilian deaths would run counter to the ultimate political aims.[6]

It is little surprise then that some dispute the wisdom of reporting deaths. In July 2010 when Wikileaks put on to the web over 92,000 US military Afghanistan logs between 2004 and 2009, a predictable debate ensued about whether this was a responsible thing to do. Nearly 150 of those logs related to civilian casualties caused by the US and its allies. They were said to show an uncomfortable reality. Beyond the deaths in themselves, what was known to the US military was that these logs had been contradicted by its own spokespersons. In addition, they were said to illustrate the reluctance to investigate assaults.[7] The scene repeated itself in October of the same year with the release of 391,832 logs for Iraq between 2004 and 2009.

And yet, claims that this material exposed the truth of cover-ups were made alongside doubt about what they had established.[8] The entries were said to be of poor quality, uncorroborated, incomplete, written in a cryptic code, or just plain false.[9] As spot assessments of what was happening on the ground, the logs were subject to the caveats typically placed on intelligence reporting.[10] As such, judgment was said to be necessary to determine whether they could be relied upon as a historical record or whether there should be doubt about what these records recorded.

Going further than the typical bounds of media coverage, it can be noted that the logs could not only be questioned for what was in them, but what was not. As military reports and assessments, they related to wounds caused by guns, explosions, etc. While injuries from direct fire are often vivid and raise the question 'Why?' they are only one way in which civilians die from conflict. Concentrating on such direct casualties – as is often the case in the news reports – can create a questionable picture. For instance, in the 1991 Persian Gulf War, direct deaths were only a fraction of those inflicted. While new 'smart' targeting weaponry enabled far more discriminate force than previous wars, this technology was directed at vital water, sanitation, power, and transportation infrastructure. One demographer attributed 110,000 indirect civilian deaths to the deterioration of facilities, in contrast to the 3,500 killed from direct fire.[11]

IGNORANCE IS STRENGTH

To understand the moves and machinations of states in depicting and defending the use of violence, this chapter examines how the UK spoke to civilian deaths stemming from the 2003 invasion of Iraq. The overall thrust of the argument is that the British officials studiously worked to avoid knowing about the number of deaths. While governments generally try to avoid being seen as ignorant, here the reverse was the case. This chapter considers the steps taken and those not taken to secure a state of unknowing.

As elsewhere in this book, the question of how revelation and concealment blend together in complex movements of transparency and secrecy will be posed. Seemingly, officials worked to conceal what they knew about what could be known about deaths. This situation frustrates the ability to make definitive claims about ignorance. Therefore, in giving an account of Iraqi deaths, this chapter examines the state of ignorance on two levels: 1) The claims made by government officials and others regarding the (im)possibility of producing fatality estimates; and 2) how those of us concerned with statecraft can know about attempts to produce ignorance.

In order to make these claims, this chapter draws on official governmental statements as well as material obtained under the 2005 UK Freedom of Information (FoI) Act. Specifically, it draws on three sets of overlapping requests made between 2008 and 2010 by the author, Richard Moyes, and another person.[12] In total, some 48 emails, letters, and other documents were obtained. The FoI Act was justified as part of the attempt to open a traditionally closed off British political system to public scrutiny. And yet, as argued elsewhere[13] and as will be evident in this case, FoI responses are characterized by limitations and vagaries that mark a highly managed form of disclosure. The plainly fractured understandings enabled by FoI responses will be used to bring to the fore some of the more commonplace difficulties of knowing about ignorance.

A CHRONOLOGY OF IGNORANCE AND AMBIGUITY

This section details the UK's responses to concerns about deaths to Iraqi civilians since 2003.

2003

Since the start of combat operations on March 20, 2003, UK officials spoke of the need to minimize *civilian casualties* and damage to *civilian* infrastructure[14] but also contended that 'it is impossible to guarantee that no civilians will be killed or injured'.[15] In response to a parliamentary question, it was also argued by the then Minister of State for the Armed Forces (Alan Ingram MP) that:

> We have made very clear our commitment to the welfare and future of the people of Iraq, and deeply regret any civilian casualties resulting from coalition action. However, it is impossible to know for sure how many civilians have been injured, or killed and subsequently buried.[16]

Ingram's assessment of 'impossibility' stood in contrast to calls at the time to establish an understanding of this issue, including a call made by 52 former senior British diplomats who wrote that 'it is a disgrace that the coalition forces themselves appear to have no estimate [of civilian casualties]'.[17]

2004

Into 2004, government officials continued to speak of the impossibility of determining the number of deaths to Iraqi civilians.[18] However, public attention to this matter intensified significantly in October when the medical journal *The Lancet* published survey results by researchers from Johns Hopkins, Columbia, and Al-Mustansiriya universities.[19] Through a technique of dividing Iraq into regions and undertaking household interviews around a 'cluster' point, the authors estimated 98,000 more Iraqis died than would have in the absence of the war (with a 95 percent confidence interval estimation range from 8,000 to 194,000). These 'excess death' estimations used a baseline mortality rate to compare death rates before and after March 2003. The authors further concluded that '[v]iolence accounted for most of the excess deaths and air strikes from coalition forces accounted for most violent deaths'.[20]

It is clear from the material released under the FoI Act that the 2004 *Lancet* study provided the spark for ministerial consideration of Iraqi civilian deaths. Although other estimates were produced in 2004,[21] these did not prompt any deliberation within Whitehall or between Whitehall and No. 10 Downing Street in the documents obtained.

In response to the 2004 *Lancet* study and the considerable media attention that followed, on November 17, 2004, the then Foreign Secretary (Jack Straw) and the then Minister of State, Foreign and Commonwealth Office (Baroness Symons) made the same statement to the House of Commons and House of Lords. This included the suggestion that:

> In many cases it would be impossible to make a reliably accurate assessment either of the civilian casualties resulting from any particular attacks or of the overall civilian casualties of a conflict. This is particularly true in the conditions that exist in Iraq.

Both asserted that hospital reports compiled by the Iraqi Ministry of Health (MoH) listing 3,853 *civilian fatalities* from 'terrorist incidents as a result of military action' between April 5, 2004 and October 5, 2004 were the 'most reliable available' tallies.

This parliamentary statement also noted that the NGO Iraq Body Count[22] provided figures that were 'an estimate relying on media reports' and which the government did 'not regard as reliable'. Despite not being reliable, the Iraq Body Count data was said to be useful because 'it does help to show however that the Iraqi Ministry of Health figures are not the only ones to differ widely from the *Lancet*'s estimate.'

These statements raise the question of what 'reliable' means, since it was said to both be impossible to derive reliable figures, but possible to specify which ones were the 'most reliable'. The situation becomes even more confusing when other statements from 2004 are noted in which it was claimed MoH figures were not 'reliable' (see Box 2.1). It would seem that after the publication of *The Lancet* report in October, the Iraqi MoH figures took on an enhanced reliability and comprehensiveness in the eyes of the British government.

Box 2.1   Unreliable but Reliable

'If the *Lancet* survey is accurate we could have expected Iraqi Ministry of Health figures, compiled by hospitals, to show many more times the number of people killed and wounded over that period than they in fact do. Hospitals in Iraq have no obvious reason to under-report the number of dead and injured'.

17 November 2004

'So while recognising the bravery and professionalism of those conducting the *Lancet* study, the Government do not accept its central conclusion, and continue to believe that the most reliable figures for casualties in Iraq are those provided by Iraqi hospitals to the Iraqi Ministry of Health'.

17 November 2004

'There are no reliable figures for Iraqi civilian deaths since March 2003. The Iraqi Ministry of Health has informed us that the number of civilians killed in security incidents is 1,203 and 3,992 wounded dating from when statistics began on 5 April 2004. However they reflect only hospital admissions and may not be comprehensive. It is not possible to break these down into how they were killed or who may have been responsible. It includes casualties caused by terrorist action'.[23]

24 June 2004

'[Iraqi Ministry of Health] statistics are not reliable, as Iraqis often bury their deceased relatives without official notification/registration. This has been particularly true during periods of heightened conflict. The MoH does not therefore have accurate figures for civilian deaths or their causes for the past year'.[24]

7 June 2004

All statements by Minister of State, Foreign and Commonwealth Office, Baroness Symons

Drawing on the material received under the FoI Act, it is possible to point to instances in which some officials appear to have sought to *manufacture ignorance* about Iraqi deaths – by disregarding data that did not suit the perceived political purpose. For instance, as part of the inter-ministerial email correspondence leading to the parliamentary statement about *The Lancet* study on November 17, 2004, one official (name and ministry withheld) referred to a poll undertaken by the International Republican Institute (IRI) which found that 22 percent of 2,000 respondents said that in the past year and a half their household had 'been directly affected by violence in terms of deaths, handicap or significant monetary loss'.[25] Another official (name and ministry withheld) responded by arguing that 'The IRI survey seems to me to harm our argument rather than help, but it is certainly useful to know'. In an email on November 9 an official likewise wrote that '22 percent of 30 million is rather a lot of people so this may back up the *Lancet's* claim, or be seen to?' In line with a desire only to muster evidence that *criticized* the 2004 *Lancet* study estimation of 98,000 deaths, it has not been possible to find the IRI's findings in any subsequent government statements.

Take another example of the manufacturing of ignorance. A 'restricted' letter from a ministry's chief economist (presumably from the FCO since it released the document) dated November 8, 2004 closed with:

It might also be possible, as Gerald Russell has suggested, to try and validate the study's pre-invasion estimate of mortality by checking it against unpublished MoH health figures. But there is (a) no certainty at this stage that this kind of work would invalidate the Lancet findings, or (b) any guarantee that if it does produce a different answer, that the rejection of the Lancet findings would be conclusive.

This quote suggests that deliberations were (again) slanted in a particular direction – towards finding grounds for rejecting *The Lancet* study. At other times in the exchanges released it could be argued that officials were not undertaking a neutral attempt to understand the impact of violence in Iraq on the civilian population. Rather – and in the absence of evidence and research of their own – they adopted the attitude of opponents to one particular study. While they did not wish to override the more nuanced evaluations of technical advisors, the general thrust of inter-ministry deliberations reads as seeking to find as many grounds as possible for dismissing *The Lancet* study's findings.

Although grounds exist for maintaining that ministry staff sought to deliberately foster ambiguity about the reliability of the *Lancet* study, it is difficult to assess and determine whether staff consciously intended to produce ignorance surrounding the study's comparatively high estimations. One complication is the difficulty of knowing what those under scrutiny knew. In this case, it is uncertain to what extent the contentions about the lack of reliable figures stemmed from the desire of officials to create doubt, or from their own lack of knowledge about the possibility of estimations. Save for fairly narrow methodological interventions by technical advisors, the 2004 deliberations obtained under the FoI action were not well informed by the history of attempts to calculate deaths in war. Repeated uncertainty and confusion was expressed about the basic statistical matters under discussion (as in Box 2.2).

Perhaps a more fundamental trouble in moving from documents to strategy is the status of language. Scholars of language today treat accounts of the world as managed descriptions given in and for particular interactional settings.[26] When language is approached as a form of social action between a sender and an audience – rather than just a means of general representation – extracting some stable, definitive meanings from words becomes problematic.[27] In this regard the quotations above, relating to a desire to find grounds against the *Lancet* estimations, need to be understood as part of ongoing internal exchanges. These are laden with mutual expectations (about literalness), taken-for-granted understandings, varying levels of trust, organizational idioms, unspoken presumptions, and so on.[28] As such – and as in the case of the 2009 leaked emails about the 'tricked' manipulation of global warming data by researchers at the University of East Anglia – arguments that some are trying to dupe others can be queried for the way meaning gets attributed 'out of context'.[29]

Furthermore, as Gilbert and Mulkay argued, attributing definitive meaning to statements presumes that 'the analyst can reconcile his version of events with all the multiple and divergent versions generated by the actors themselves'.[30] In other words, individuals can say contrasting things; sometimes related to different forms of communication (for instance, formal writing, informal collegial banter, interviews, or emails). Those who take it as their role to decipher what is really meant must find a way of sorting this diversity. Often this is done by establishing 'linguistic consistency'.

Box 2.2   Displays of Ignorance

Of note in the correspondence obtained under the FoI Act is the *level of ignorance* of officials. Repeatedly within the correspondence obtained under the FoI, officials expressed uncertainty about the issues at hand. Consider in this regard the quote below, part of inter-ministerial email correspondence leading the November 17, 2004 House of Commons and Lords statements about the *Lancet* study:

From: ▇▇▇▇▇▇▇▇▇▇▇▇▇▇▇▇
Sent: 07 November 2004 14:29
To: ▇▇▇▇▇▇▇▇▇▇▇▇▇▇▇▇▇▇▇▇▇▇▇▇
Cc: ▇▇▇▇▇▇▇▇▇▇▇▇▇▇▇▇▇
Subject: RE: Foreign Secretary's draft statement on civilian casualties

> I'm still worried about where we may be heading. Obviously if the estimate of 100,000 is wrong, we must make that clear. But for every flaw identified, there is testament to the study's sound methodology. The Economist quoted Scott Zeger, head of department of biostatistics at Johns Hopkins that the clustered sampling is the rule in public health studies. Death by epidemic also varies by location. If this is how these people usually calculate the effects of epidemics, we need to be careful about criticising it, especially when we have made no attempt of our own to make an estimate – a very major weakness. And I still suspect someone somewhere either has a rough estimate, or the means to pull one together from different pieces of evidence and reporting. If it one day emerges under FAC questioning for example, thayt [sic] someone in the Mod or FCO though [sic] the number were higher than we've acknowledged, we would deservedly face public criticism.

This passage makes a number of points echoed elsewhere:

(a) the UK made no official effort of its own to estimate civilian deaths and (at least) some regarded this as a deficiency;
(b) the 2004 *Lancet* study's methodology was subject to both negative and positive assessments within Whitehall. So with regard to the latter, in the FoI material released the MOD's Chief Scientific Adviser concluded that the 'design of the study is robust' and a chief economist (presumably from the FCO, see below) assessed that its methodology 'appears sound', although both also offered some grounds for reservation about the 98,000 figure;
(c) among many of those drawing up official statements, knowledge of the methodological issues at stake appear rather limited; and
(d) major public statements were crafted despite backstage acknowledgement of ignorance regarding what was known by government departments.

As Gilbert and Mulkay suggest, what is taken as 'really meant' is that which is in line with the overall thrust of the arguments put forward. As a result, some statements are taken at face value while others are disregarded. Moving from a position of noting that officials were dubious about the *Lancet*'s claims to accusing officials of manufacturing deliberate doubt would require sidelining other statements made by officials, such as those that referred to a 'genuine judgment' that no reliable methodology was possible and that the *Lancet* study was 'straight from the department of guesswork'.[31] Not only would such discounting be questionable, it would run counter to a central concern from Chapter 1: the importance of attending to how statements are offered on specific occasions.

If these difficulties, stemming from the treatment of language as social action, pose challenges in general, then these are all the more acutely experienced when information restrictions are imposed. Most of the names, many of the positions, and some organizational affiliations were redacted from the FoI-released documentation.[32] Such conditions of partial disclosure frustrate the hope that government openness leads to comprehension.

To complicate matters still further, it appears that some of those preparing official responses recognized a need for strategic management of what was said. An internal Foreign and Commonwealth Office (FCO) letter sent to No. 10 Downing Street on October 14, 2004 stated:

> The US have, like ourselves, stuck to the line that there are no comprehensive figures for civilian casualties and do not comment on suggested figures. The Embassy in Washington has asked for the US's official estimate of civilian casualties in Iraq. We still await the responses from the State Department and Department of Defense.
>
> In sum, if we produce a figure that differs from the Iraqi government figures, we will have to defend it – and the way it was arrived at – before parliament and the media. ▮▮▮▮▮▮▮▮▮ ▮▮▮▮▮▮▮▮▮▮▮▮▮▮▮▮▮▮▮▮▮▮▮▮. We recommend that for the moment we continue to put our public emphasis on specific atrocities against civilians, such as the mass killing of Iraqi children in Baghdad on 30 September, and their attempts to thwart our efforts to stand up independent Iraqi security forces.[33]

This passage would seem to indicate this FCO official (a) recognized the possibility that the US and the UK could derive civilian casualty estimates; (b) believed the US had already produced one; (c) was unaware of the estimation; (d) thought it was best to maintain a public line that it was not possible to derive a comprehensive figure; and (e) thought it best to focus on atrocities committed by others.[34] With regard to (d), it was recognized that producing figures might require defending them. The passage is suggestive of not treating government statements at face value because at least some individuals saw the need for calculative rhetorical defenses.[35]

In light of this analysis of the FoI material, it is possible to develop a refined understanding of the November 17, 2004 parliamentary statements regarding the 2004 *Lancet* study mentioned above. In these statements by the then Foreign Secretary (Jack Straw), and the then Minister of State, Foreign and Commonwealth Office (Baroness Symons), the criticism of this study concentrated on 'the accuracy of the data' subject to analysis. Both voiced concerns about the small sample size, the overall 'limited precision' of the data, and the difficulty of accurately attributing who was responsible for deaths. The divergence between this study and the Iraqi MoH numbers was also said to bring grounds for questioning the former (although it was not noted that these contrasting figures were measuring different types of deaths).

In criticizing the study at the level of its *data* (rather than its methodology, for instance), it was possible for ministers to reject its estimate of some 98,000 deaths without doubting the cluster sampling *method*; a rejection that government technical advisors warned against. Yet, as a by-product of this line of argument, focusing on data at least opened the possibility that the cluster sampling method could yield reliable figures in the future (*if* the data could be improved), although this sat uneasily with the aforementioned claims that reliable figures were simply 'impossible' in the case of Iraq.

In choosing to criticize *The Lancet* study rather than offer any estimates of their own, positive criteria for judging estimates, or recommendations for what type of research was necessary, ministers were able to deflect attention away from the uncertainties and disagreements within Whitehall that are evident from the FoI-released material.

2006

Despite this public and parliamentary interest at the end of 2004, according to the FoI-released material obtained, it was not until late 2006 that the level of Iraqi deaths from armed violence again became a matter of UK Government deliberation. Once again, this was in response to a survey led by researchers at Johns Hopkins University that appeared in the medical journal *The Lancet*. Published on October 12, 2006, this second survey gave an average estimate of the number of excess Iraqis deaths at 654,965 (based on an estimated range between 392,979 to 942,636 with a 95 percent confidence interval).[36]

The Guardian newspaper reported that on the day of its release the Prime Minister's official spokesman rejected the study's conclusions by saying:

> The problem with this is that they are using an extrapolation technique from a relatively small sample, from an area of Iraq which isn't representative of the country as a whole. We have questioned that technique right from the beginning and we continue to do so. The Lancet figure is an order of magnitude higher than any other figure; it is not one we believe to be anywhere near accurate ... There is a democratically-elected, sovereign government [in Iraq] and therefore it is for the Iraqi government – as would be entirely the case in the United Kingdom – to address these issues and not for us.[37]

On October 19, 2006 the Parliamentary Under-Secretary of State, Foreign and Commonwealth Office, Lord Triesman, offered a less strident negative assessment in a prepared statement to the House of Lords:

> My Lords, every civilian death is a tragedy and must be of concern in Iraq, as elsewhere. However, we continue to believe that there are no comprehensive or reliable figures for deaths since 2003. Estimates vary according to the method of collection. The figure of 655,000 given in the recent *Lancet* survey is significantly higher than other estimates, including those provided by the Iraqi Government. We believe that the Iraqi Government are best placed to monitor deaths among their own civilians.[38]

The interesting elements in this response are its continuities and discontinuities with previous statements. Whilst there is a recognition that methodologies differ, there is again no recognition that different methodologies were measuring different types of death.

As noted in the previous subsection, earlier official responses to the 2004 *Lancet* study focused on the data inputted into the methodology and how its results were out of line with other estimates. While attention to the latter was maintained in 2006, Lord Triesman made no reference to the underlying data.

Through the FoI releases, it is possible to speculate about the causes and consequences for this omission. Similar to 2004, this material indicates civil servant advisors (from the Department for International Development (DfID) and the Ministry of Defence (MoD) in 2006) recommended against criticizing the *Lancet* study's methodological design (as seemingly done in the statement above by the Prime Minister's official spokesman).[39] In the case of the DfID advisor, grounds were given for why the 2006 *Lancet* study might have *underestimated* mortality. In addition, the advisors noted improvements to the data obtained, including the larger sample sizes, sampling techniques, and the use of improved and death-certificate verification. When these advisers' appraisals about methodological soundness later got out to the press, they were seized upon as evidence of government skullduggery.[40]

By not noting the improvements made to the data, the official statement by Lord Triesman failed to acknowledge how the 2006 *Lancet* study redressed 2004 ministerial criticisms. The very brevity of the statement,[41] though, arguably frustrates efforts to assess the grounds offered for Lord Triesman's evaluation.

As another point of contrast between 2004 and 2006, instead of the (qualified) endorsement of Iraqi Ministry of Health figures, in 2006 Lord Triesman contended that 'Estimates vary according to the method of collection'. This shift to a kind of methodological pluralism meant that the quality of the *data* in 2006 was diminished as a relevant consideration since the data were not the (only) source for the divergent death-figures. Yet, adopting this stance brought critical questioning during a debate in the House of Lords:

Lord Marsh: My Lords, does the Minister agree that the methodology of this study was unique in the way in which it was pursued? It is difficult to see how the Government can take the line, 'The study was done in a way which is well known, and it was done very well, but we don't think that it is worth very much'. Lord Triesman: My Lords, that is not the view that I have put at all. I said that there are different methods which have arrived at very different figures and that those methods also are legitimate. The way in which data are extrapolated from samples to a general outcome is a matter of deep concern and merits considerable study rather than the denunciation of one method compared with another.[42]

In pointing to the 'deep concern', the response by Lord Triesman appears to open up statistical methodologies to questioning in a manner that they were arguably not subject to during the 2004 official parliamentary statements. In the latter, the quality of the data was the source of concern – although again what is being discussed might well be regarded as unclear because of its brevity.

Just what Lord Triesman's statements should be taken to mean overall for the standing of death estimates is difficult to comprehend. The monitoring of deaths was deemed a responsibility of the Iraqi government, and therefore, presumably, doable at some level. As such, ignorance was framed in a way that implied further knowledge was attainable.[43] And yet, the suggestions of methodological pluralism undermined the prospects of sorting out these equally legitimate tallies. In this thinking it might be said, following Norris, that the dead became 'objects of *deconstruction*, figures impossible to verify and locate and therefore incapable of serving any intellectual operation other than that of [signaling] the impossibility of determining their reality'.[44]

What does seem certain is that in practice the need for 'considerable study' mentioned in Lord Triesman's reply was not part of an announcement that the UK would be commissioning such work.[45]

2007

Parliamentary and public concern about Iraqi deaths continued into 2007. A statement by Kim Howells, Secretary of State for Foreign and Commonwealth Affairs, on the October 9, 2007 provided the latest version of the UK position:

The Government do not collate figures for civilian casualties in Iraq. The Government of Iraq is best placed to monitor the numbers of Iraqi civilian casualties, but we continue to believe that there are no comprehensive or reliable figures for deaths since March 2003 as estimates vary according to the method of collection.[46]

In making these contentions, the Secretary restated themes made by Lord Triesman in 2006, namely that the Iraqi government was the one that should be monitoring deaths and that the variability of results by method meant that there were no comprehensive or reliable figures.

The FoI Act released information obtained for 2007 that included only two linked types of material: an email chain between a couple of FCO officials and one official from DfID, along with an FCO checklist. The December email exchanges appear to have pertained to a government Public Service Agreement regarding international conflict prevention and resolution. As part of this attention to reducing the burden of conflict, an official from the FCO Iraq Group was tasked with compiling a bullet-point checklist of the different measures of Iraqi civilian deaths, an appraisal of their reliability, and the official UK statements made about them.

As with previously cited FoI material, the 2007 material raises basic concerns about the ignorance of British officials, particularly in relation to error and uncertainty. In relation to error, for instance, the December 7 two-page checklist (titled 'Analysis of Iraqi Civilian Death Tolls') included the following evaluations about the 2004 *Lancet* study:

Advantages:
  • None
Disadvantages:
  • Methodology deemed flawed by MOD's Chief Scientific Adviser and FCO's Chief Economist

However, in the internal letters obtained by the author, while certain critical points were raised (mainly relating to data), the MOD's chief scientific adviser judged that the 'design of the study is robust' and a 'chief economist' noted above (presumably from the Foreign Office) concluded that the statistical methodology 'appears sound'.

In relation to concerns about uncertainty, the checklist document suggested the basis for some Iraq government figures was unknown to the UK. For both the Iraqi MoI figures and joint Iraqi Ministry of Interior, Health, and Defence figures, it was written that no details were provided about how they were put together.[47] So despite the UK proposing the Iraq government was best placed to monitor deaths, it did not know how the latter's estimates were derived.

And yet, while it seems appropriate to label these as instances of error and uncertainty, such characterizations may be ill judged; especially as, given what seems to be the lack of knowledge displayed across the civil service regarding Iraqi deaths, the uncertainty about the Iraqi government methods for compiling death figures might well stem from sheer confusion.

2008

Early in 2008, the *New England Journal of Medicine* published a survey undertaken by a variety of Iraqi organizations in collaboration with the World Health Organization.[48] Based on interviews, that survey estimated that from March 2003 to June 2006, 151,000

Iraqis[49] – combatants and civilians – had died from violent deaths. The study did not include deaths from accident, disease, or suicide as did the *Lancet* studies.

It does not appear that this new study initiated any discussion or analysis in Whitehall. No material dated from 2008 onwards was released as part of the FoI requests. A House of Commons parliamentary question in February 2008 about dead Iraqis brought a reference back to the previously cited October 9, 2007 statement by the Secretary of State for Foreign and Commonwealth Affairs in which he said:

> The Government do not collate figures for civilian casualties in Iraq. The Government of Iraq is best placed to monitor the numbers of Iraqi civilian casualties, but we continue to believe that there are no comprehensive or reliable figures for deaths since March 2003 as estimates vary according to the method of collection.[50]

Thus, in keeping with previous years, there is no recognition by British government ministers in public statements that the Iraqi government might be compromised in its ability to monitor deaths – either because of lack of capacity, internal divisions or political constraints. However, a number of commentators at the time did propose that internal and external political pressures on Iraq and its agencies resulted in civilian death tallies not being produced or being underestimated.[51]

If there was no suggestion in official statements from 2008 or elsewhere of the possible politics of mortality figures, neither was there an acknowledgement in official statements or FoI-released material that the British government should have intervened to ensure figures were produced. So, despite the UK becoming an occupying power in 2003, its calls for Iraqi government action were seemingly empty.

2010

Public attention to civilian deaths in the UK was rekindled in 2009–10 with the initiation of the official 'Iraq Inquiry'. The substantial hearings, testimonies, and evidence-gathering undertaken as part of this inquiry were meant to identify lessons for the future. As part of the testimony to the Inquiry, on January 29, 2010, former Prime Minister Tony Blair stated:

when people say, 'There were people dying in Iraq', and, you know, the figures, I think the most reliable figures out of the Iraq Body Count or the Brookings Institute may be 100,000 over this whole period – the coalition forces weren't the ones doing the killing. The ones doing the killing were the terrorists, the sectarians, and they were doing it quite deliberately to stop us making the progress we wanted to make.

In making this statement, he both continued and broke with previous official statements. As before, he acknowledged the problem of casualties, but sought to deflect attention away from deaths resulting from the actions of the UK and its partners – either direct conflict deaths or indirect casualties stemming from the loss of vital infrastructure.

As before, Tony Blair did not offer any official British government figures for the number of civilians killed since 2003. The reason for this is simple: the UK never produced any. Neither did it act to support the production of officially recognized figures by others. So, despite the many words of sympathy repeatedly voiced by ministers, it is difficult to identify structured efforts to analyze and reduce civilian casualties from military operations in Iraq. This is not to say that, at a local level, UK troops were not choosing tactics or making decisions in a way that considered the risk to civilians. Rather, it is to highlight shortcomings in the overarching framework under which the risks were assessed and approached in the case of Iraq. The offices of Whitehall were seemingly unaware of basic points about how the *multi-national force* assessed deaths associated with its actions in practice.

As before, Tony Blair cited those findings that gave comparatively low estimates for *civilian* deaths – and figures measuring *only* direct violence deaths – when pressed in questioning. However, by citing Iraq Body Count and the 'Brookings Institute' [sic Institution] estimations the former Prime Minster did depart from past practices of UK ministry officials and ministers. The Iraq Body Count was frequently criticized in backstage inter-ministry deliberations obtained under the FoI. The former Foreign Secretary Jack Straw said he did 'not regard [them] as reliable'. The Brooking Institution's 'Iraq Index' (itself complied from the Iraq Body Count and other primary sources[52]) was only once mentioned in passing once within the Whitehall correspondence I obtained.

What prompted the rethink about these two tolls for Blair is unclear. Nothing in the information obtained would suggest reasons why the government assessment of them should change in this way. It seems likely that Blair's citation reflects the expedient manner, since 2003, that certain figures were latched on to as and when it served the situation.

So, while citing these particular figures marked a break with the past, Blair continued with the makeshift manner in which certain numbers were favored in an attempt to reduce anxiety about deaths to civilians.

ATTRIBUTING IGNORANCE

In reflecting on how civilians die in combat, Hugo Slim offered a three-part breakdown of how deaths have been made sense of by political leaders: 1) as a desirable end; 2) as a means to an end; and 3) as an undesired outcome. In relation to the final 'regretful' position he argued that 'to prove civilian suffering was coincidental or accidental as opposed to a violation, military forces need to be able to show clearly what they know, what they could have known, what they did and what they could have done'.[53]

This chapter has considered one government that presented casualties from its use of force in a regretful tone. By its own standards, the UK should have sought to understand the levels of civilian harm resulting from its actions in Iraq – but it did not. Rather than attempting to show clearly what they knew, what they could have known, what they did, and what they could have done, this chapter has argued that UK officials ended up being unclear about what they knew and dismissive about what they could have known, as well as elusive about what they did and did not do.

With no figures of its own, British government responses about what could be known regarding civilians deaths stemming from the 2003 Iraq war included claiming that no reliable figures existed, 'reliable' figures were impossible to derive, some figures were more 'reliable' than others, some figures were more unreliable than others, different methodologies led to different tolls, and the job of producing figures was one for the Iraqi government.

This chapter has contrasted the twists and turns of public statements against back-region government and civil-service deliberations. In doing so, 'covering moves'[54] by government officials to scientific studies have been identified. These were likely to foment ignorance by:

- Seeking to raise doubts about only certain types of figures;
- Not acknowledging information that ran counter to this end;

- Proposing the need for meta-studies not then supported;
- Changing positions in unremarked-upon ways; and
- Using ambiguous terminology.

It has been possible to speculate about what these tactics have meant for political accountability. Ambiguity in meaning, for instance, served to render it difficult for outsiders to know what was known by government officials. It also enabled the carpeting over of internal ministerial disagreement and unawareness.[55]

And yet, for all the ways in which this analysis opens the UK government up to charges of manufacturing doubt, the previous section has also sought to consider problems with analysts attributing and characterizing ignorance-production strategies. The rest of this chapter extends these points.

In relation to the topic of what officials knew, the incompleteness of data stifles the determination of what took place. While the FoI-released material obtained provided glimpses into otherwise closed-off bureaucratic deliberations, that these are only partial glimpses undermines any attempt to determine their import and character. While many documents were made available, it is clear from ministerial responses that others were not.

Moreover, as this analysis drew on material from three overlapping sets of FoI requests it has been possible to get a sense of the variability in what becomes made public. For instance, ministries made available documents that pertained to other ministries that the latters did not release. In other cases, documents released under more than one request had different redacted elements.[56] Sometimes email exchanges and documents were released with redacted elements blacked out, at other times portions of 'relevant' text were cut and pasted into compilations.

In short then, access to some information has suggested grounds for the partiality of that information. Such a condition should raise questions regarding the limitations of any depictions of events made from FoI released.[57] But more generally, this recognition raises questions about how social analysis can take place in situations of partial disclosure. With its glaring redactions and exemptions imposed by a formal system of control, the FoI makes explicit the conditions of partial information experienced more widely in examining statecraft. How to characterize and give a place to that which remains unknown is as problematic as it is prevalent.[58]

However, it is not simply the case that the problems of attributing ignorance strategies are derived from incompleteness of empirical data. The difficulties go far beyond certain material being blacked out. Instead, the 'back region' correspondence obtained added another set of material that had to be made sense of in relation to the production of ignorance. So in this case, the correspondence obtained gave reasons to wonder whether officials were deliberately fashioning doubt or whether they were ignorant themselves of the issues at hand.

One way of handling such difficulties of meaning-making would be to take a position on the real facts and then use that to interpret individuals' actions. For instance, in their examination of ignorance production, Oreskes and Conway start with the reality of human-caused global warming in order to question why, and catalogue how, skeptics are seeking to fabricate dubious doubt.[59] In relation to the topic of this chapter, it would be possible to side with a particular type of estimation in order to critically evaluate claims to the contrary.[60]

Yet, reading back from 'the facts' in order to decipher who is trying to produce ignorance has severe limits. For one, it highly restricts the range of topics, when they can be studied, and who can credibly do this. Also, starting with an understanding of which claims are true and which claims are false threatens to flatten out a sense how, as part of the unfolding controversy, claims were advanced about what could be known or was known. In the case examined here, while individuals traded certain terminology and evaluations as part of a debate, it is not at all clear whether the meaning of what was said was mutually shared. While the ambiguity of key terms – such as what constitutes 'reliable' – provides an analytical locus for the negotiated management of meaning, that ambiguity thwarts specifying what was happening in detail. Stated bluntly, the conditions that suggest the production of ignorance also frustrate the specifying of it.

Because of this 'uncertainty about disagreement', it is necessary to consider a second-level order of ignorance involved in the study of ignorance: how the lack of certainty about the issues disputed should lead to doubt about what is being doubted in the first place. In this situation of uncertainty about ignorance, it is questionable to try to characterize 'what was going on' and 'what was meant by what was said' through drawing on a predetermined sense of 'the facts'.

Overall then, the case of Iraqi deaths has been used to suggest what some of the difficulties associated with knowing about the manufacture of ignorance might be. Specifying this requires tackling varied conceptual and practical quandaries. As part of this, it should be recognized that those wishing to attribute ignorance can end up employing many of the same argumentative techniques as those studied here, such as brushing over ambiguities in the use of words, focusing on certain statements over others, making questionable presumptions to assign meaning, and offering definite claims in conditions of partial knowledge. Those too could be questioned in terms of how they promote ignorance.

3
Disabling Discourses: International Law, Legitimacy, and the Politics of Balance

The previous chapters have considered major areas of controversy associated with the 2003 Iraq war and elsewhere. The examination of how evaluations of spin were made, and how fatality figures were produced, threw into question what should be regarded as hidden, within view, obscured, and transparent. Trying to make sense of the world of statecraft could be likened to trying to discern the source of an intricate scene of flickering shadows.

As argued, the scenes on display were produced by the shared and limited terms of debate. In the case of WMD reporting, that meant (among other things) a discussion about the faithfulness of words that did not attend to how faithfulness was established. In the case of Iraqi deaths that meant (among other things) a discussion about estimates that did not ask what was being estimated. Party to the collective stifling of imagination were government officials, political reporters, policy analysts, academics, and others. Each asserted the 'facts of the matter' with little consideration of the basis for these claims.

Rather than revealing the reality behind the appearances of shadows, in recognition of the elusiveness possible in grasping what is going on, my analysis so far has sought to attend to what gets taken as real. This chapter goes a step further by asking how the questioning of what is known could provide a basis for understanding and for intervention into the practices of statecraft. It does so in relation to the international legal rules that govern armed conflict.

INTERNATIONAL HUMANITARIAN LAW

The history of attempts to establish the 'limits at which the necessities of war ought to yield to the requirements of humanity'[1] is perhaps as old as the recorded history of conflict itself. While some might define it as the suspension of restraint, this is not how warfare is regarded under the law today. Particularly after the large-scale atrocities of World War II, efforts were made to restrict the conduct of conflict through international law.[2] That has included devising rules about when force is a legitimate resort and what protections should be given to victims and prisoners.

This chapter considers another aspect of international law: limits on the means and methods of warfare. Article 35(1) of the 1977 First Additional Protocol to the Geneva Conventions of 1949 lays out one basic tenet in stating: 'In any armed conflict, the right of the Parties to the conflict to choose methods or means of warfare is not unlimited'. Those limits are set out in numerous treaties and customary law.[3]

Central to the parts of international humanitarian law (IHL) applicable to the conduct of armed conflict is a basic obligation: the needs of military necessity must be balanced by concerns for humanity. This balancing is embodied in a number of specific legal rules, such as the rules regarding superfluous injury and unnecessary suffering, environmental protection, distinction, indiscriminate attacks, and feasible precautions.[4] The call for a balancing between military necessity and humanity is most straightforwardly relevant to the rule of proportionality. This sets out that:

Who: Military commanders[5] (perhaps with assistance from legal advisors[6])
What: Determine what force is permissible for legitimate objects of attack
When: On a case-by-case basis[7]
How: By 'carefully considering'[8] anticipated incidental loss of civilian life and damage to civilian property against the anticipated military advantage.

Whether and how this cost–benefit logic for understanding and evaluating force can be applied are the topics of this chapter.[9] This will be done by considering IHL in relation to a specific case, that of 'cluster bombs' (or 'cluster munitions').

CLUSTER MUNITIONS: LEGAL AND BALANCED

Cluster munitions are ground- or air-launched weapon systems. They consist of a large metal casing that contains multiple (up to hundreds) explosive submunitions. After being fired, the submunitions are released and disperse over an area, typically from several hundred to many thousands of square meters.

For over 40 years, some governments, NGOs, international organizations, and others have voiced concerns about the humanitarian consequences from cluster munitions in places such as Lao, Cambodia, Vietnam, Lebanon, Western Sahara, Chechnya, Ethiopia, Eritrea, Afghanistan, and Iraq. The problems identified with them in recent years have been two-fold: 1) the often large area affected means they can strike both military and civilian objects; and 2) the failure of the submunitions to explode as intended presents a post-conflict unexploded ordnance threat as they can be set off if disturbed. When this happens the result is injury, dismemberment, or death. Box 3.1 illustrates the types of concerns assqciated with injuries inflicted.

Box 3.1   Cluster Munitions in Kosovo and the former Yugoslavia

In advance of the bombing of Kosovo in 1999, non-governmental organizations appealed to NATO not to use cluster munitions because of the excessive civilian harm from these weapons evidenced in previous conflicts.[10] However, the representatives of NATO states effectively denied that any particular problems were associated with these weapons and used them in large quantities and in areas of civilian concentration. Some 380,000 submunitions were dropped by NATO forces. All of the main cluster munition types used had established histories of unreliability.

Casualties were documented during the bombing as a result of inaccurate attacks and the area affect of cluster munitions striking civilians as well as military targets.[11]

According to data from the International Committee of the Red Cross (ICRC), in the year after the bombing cluster munitions were responsible for some 82 percent of accidents from all types of unexploded ordnance.[12] This despite repeated assertions by NATO political and military representatives that cluster munitions were just the same as other weapons in creating an unexploded ordnance threat. Data from the ICRC suggested that cluster munitions were more akin to landmines in their post-conflict impact:

> Cluster bomblets and anti-personnel mines accounted for 73% of the 280 incidents individually recorded by the ICRC between 1 June 1999 to 31 May, 2000, with each type of ordnance responsible for 102 deaths or injuries ... In addition, as compared to those killed or injured by anti-personnel mines, those injured or killed by cluster bombs were 4.9 times as likely to be under age 14.[13]

▶

The ICRC also cast doubt on the veracity of NATO estimations of the number of cluster submunitions that failed to detonate, suggesting the overall reliability rate was between 10 and 15 percent. As in other conflicts, the overall and type-specific failure rates of unexploded ordnance were matters of significant disagreement between inter-governmental organizations, NGOs, and government officials.[14]

Other sources of concern were noted by the ICRC, including the use of CBU-87 out of warranty, the failure to employ self-destruction mechanisms, and the questionable accuracy of some attacks. In addition, cluster munitions were said to pose a unique challenge for disposal operations because of their sensitive fuses, the need for *in situ* destruction, the inability to use mechanical clearance techniques, and the frequency with which they penetrated the soil.

That the level of casualties from cluster munitions dropped very rapidly immediately after the conflict was substantially related to the very high levels of investment in mine action in the region. According to the Landmine Monitor Report 2002: '[an] evaluation concluded that a total of about $85 million had been invested in the mine action program in Kosovo from mid-1999 to the end of 2001'.[15] Despite these high levels of investment, cluster munitions continued to be cleared in Kosovo some years after the conflict.

Given the amount and duration of attention to this type of weapon, cluster munitions could be regarded as something of a 'best case' for asking how IHL bears on conflict. Indeed, major user states frequently argue that cluster munitions have been tested against the law and have been used in accordance with the law. The extensive firing of cluster munitions in Lebanon by Israeli forces in 2006 was perhaps the most controversial usage in recent times.[16] With four million submunitions fired into South Lebanon, with an estimated failure rate of 25 percent, the immediate and post-war effects of these weapons was significant.[17] Against international outcry – such as the conclusion by a team of UN special rapporteurs that judged their firing as 'reckless, perhaps even deliberately reckless'[18] – Israel maintained that 'the use of cluster munitions is not prohibited by international law ... [t]his weapon is used by a number of states and, as in the case of all arms, the use of cluster munitions must conform to the rules of warfare'.[19] While (what is publicly known about) two internal Israeli investigations offered certain critical points about the 2006 attacks into Lebanon, they concluded that Israel's use of cluster munitions was as a whole consistent with IHL and that these weapons were not banned under international law.[20]

At times governments have gone further than stating these weapons were permissible. In 2008, as the world's largest stockpiler and user, the United States, argued against calls for an international ban by contending that 'the blanket elimination of cluster munitions is unacceptable due not only to negative military consequences but also due to the potential negative consequences for civilians'.[21] The reasoning was that once banned, militaries would have to resort to unitary weapons that 'could result in some cases, in unacceptable collateral damage and explosive remnants'.[22]

While cluster munitions had been subject to international attention since the Vietnam War, between 2001 and 2006 official state-level consideration of their legality took place within the UN Convention on Certain Conventional Weapons (CCW).[23] Colloquially known as the 'Inhumane Weapon Convention', the CCW is tasked with examining whether weapons are excessively injurious or have indiscriminate effects. During this timeframe, governments repeatedly maintained that cluster munitions, as a category of weapons, were legally permissible. While they might be used irresponsibly, they were otherwise legal. States differed on whether the weapons posed significant humanitarian concerns and what should be done. Russia, for instance, maintained that cluster munitions should not be associated with any distinctive concerns.[24] The US, along with many other countries, called for the destruction of certain unreliable stockpiles and for technical improvements, while simultaneously arguing against anything remotely approaching a categorical ban.[25] Others spoke of revisiting targeting practices – such as the appropriateness of high-altitude bombing[26] or their firing into populated areas.[27] By early 2006, only the Holy See and Mexico had endorsed the idea of a moratorium on their use.

Such political positions were in line with legal analysis at the time. With the basic logic of weighing military advantage versus civilian damage on a case-by-case basis, an outright ban would be difficult to justify through IHL. Doing so would require judging that the harm to civilians would be excessive across expected use scenarios. One point of note is that this would have been highly demanding. As argued by Christopher Greenwood QC, in a legal analysis for the UK government at the CCW, the 'whole picture' of the effects of different weapons would need to be examined when considering what to do about cluster munitions. If this did not happen 'it may be that the protection of the civilian population is diminished rather than enhanced'.[28] A second point to note is that the justification for an outright ban would be highly unlikely given the varied conditions in which cluster munitions could be used as well as the varied types of weapons.

As a result, since the time they came to international attention, few detailed legal assessments argued cluster munitions were unlawful under IHL.[29] Instead, lawyers and scholars shared with many states the importance of reform measures to get rid of 'legacy munitions' with a high failure rate, to improve targeting practices, and to undertake other modifications intended to get rid of the 'worst of the worst'.

Some lawyers and governments also called for a clarification of IHL so that what went into the balancing of military necessity versus humanity could be settled. As part of this, the proposal was forwarded that the likely long-term effects of submunitions should be taken into account.[30] This was not the position of the US, Russia, Israel, or the UK though.

Likewise, with little exception, prior to 2006 NGOs, UN agencies, and other humanitarian-minded organizations stopped short of calling for an outright ban.[31] Major commentators such as Human Rights Watch, the ICRC, Landmine Action, and others pitched their concerns through the 'weighing' requirements of IHL.

EVIDENCE AND ARGUMENT

The principles and rules of IHL then provided the dominant means of making sense of whether cluster munitions were permissible. Because IHL stipulates the need for 'balancing', the facts about civilian damage and military advantage matter. Which facts (Do long term civilian harms count?) and whose facts (Dud rate claims by manufacturers or field demining organizations?) were disputed, but such information was taken as the basis for decision making. In theory, understanding the 'whole' picture of the comparative effects of cluster munitions required knowing about complicated matters such as dud rates across different terrains and conditions, the likelihood of casualties, and the possibility for removing any post-war remnants.[32]

The ease of calculating the balance of such varied factors was something that legal scholars presented as more[33] or less[34] straight-forward. As with so many other points in the chapters of this book, the prospect for striking a balance was subjected to multiple portrayals – even by the same individuals. While appearing before the House of Commons Select Committee on Defence, the former

Secretary of Defence Geoff Hoon rejected the idea that the UK had a distorted prioritization between the safety of its military and civilians in this exchange:

> Mr Hoon: We were aware that there was a small failure rate, in the order of five per cent, estimated by the manufacturers as far as cluster bombs were concerned, but a judgment has to be made. These are extremely effective weapons. They are the most effective weapons against armoured and certain kinds of soft skinned vehicles and, frankly, if we did not use the most effective weapons available to us we would be putting our armed forces at risk. I would face, rightly, criticism from this Committee if, in an exercise such as we are conducting now, I did not use a weapon that was available to us and our armed forces were put at risk in the process.
>
> Mr Cohen: How many refugees and innocent civilians is a pilot worth?
>
> Mr Hoon: I do not think it is proper for me to try and deal with that.
>
> Mr Cohen: In your assessment?
>
> Mr Hoon: Judgments are made. Military campaigns inevitably involve risk both for the armed forces of this country and, indeed, for civilians of other countries. That is something which is taken into account which is why we take account of relevant principles of international law both in terms of the targets that we select and, indeed, in terms of the equipment that we utilise.[35]

When pressed under testimony this political leader suggested something less than a neat, certain, and tidy formula for striking the balance required under the law.[36] This exchange stands in contrast to less qualified statements made elsewhere by Hoon that made no allowance for any inexpressibles or incalculables.[37]

Yet, whatever the acknowledged messiness, the repeated contention was that the weighing was taking place.

THE FOG OF (THE LAWS OF) WAR

To the substantial controversy surrounding the use of cluster munitions since the 1960s, user and stockpiler nations offered confident assurances to their populations and to each other that these weapons were legal in general and were used in a legal manner (expect in a very few instances involving non-Western forces[38]).

This section sets out reasons for supporting an alternative argument: that government proclamations to the effect that 'the rules were followed' hid a basic ignorance. The issue is not one of how 'calculations' were made or inputs prioritized, but rather the fundamental one of whether any kind of informed balance was being undertaken.

In making this case, the aim is to question the shared bounds of international debate. Take the US. In a 2005 report, the Defense Science Board Task Force of the US Department of Defense was charged with examining future options to ensure the reliability of munitions. The Task Force concluded it could 'identify no comprehensive approach – empirical observation or otherwise – to determine and document operational combat failure rates of U.S. munitions ... There is no method in place that can systematically determine and document the reliability rates of a broad range of munitions during combat'.[39] In response to such identified failures, the Task Force called for measures such as the development of robust assessment methodologies; research and development into new fuses, target identification, and guidance systems; and reforms in acquisition procedures. The report was presented at the CCW in 2005 as part of the suggestion that the US was taking the necessary reformist measures.

What the *Munitions System Reliability* report failed to draw any attention to was the disparity between its analysis and the long history of confident public and diplomatic statements made by US officials regarding: 1) the reliable performance of its cluster munitions; and 2) the said exaggeration of humanitarian fears.[40] Without informed determinations of in-field reliability though, it is difficult to imagine how commanders could operate in anything like the measured manner portrayed. This would be the case whatever else the US did by way of assessing effects – such as purportedly employing a computer program to make determinations of the pro-portionality of attacks in Iraq.[41]

Take another major user country where a fuller picture of ignorance can be sketched: the UK. In late 2005, in a report titled *Out of Balance,* I analyzed official government statements between 1990 and 2005 for the NGO Landmine Action. The purpose was to build a comprehensive understanding of what information the UK had on the humanitarian effects of cluster munitions.[42] Its conclusions were stark: the UK had undertaken no practical assessments of the humanitarian consequences of cluster munitions during the time period examined, despite the extent of public controversy.

Furthermore, it had not collected data on the details of submunitions discovered in its post-conflict ordnance disposal operations or the failure rates of its submunitions in combat situations. Instead of compiling field data of its own, officials repeated the comparatively low failure rate claims of manufacturers in order to discredit claims from civil society. On the back of *Out of Balance*, Landmine Action worked with those in the House of Commons and the Lords on follow-up questions for the government. The responses reaffirmed the absences of evidence and the absence of attempts to gather evidence.

Some media coverage of *Out of Balance* suggested that it meant Britain was 'finally being held to account'[43] over its use of cluster munitions in Iraq. Yet the report itself was overwhelmingly based on open-source material long available. It was only able to be produced because of the hundreds of references to cluster munitions in parliament and elsewhere prompted by longstanding humanitarian concerns. To the extent that it offered anything novel, it brought together various strains of information. If this report could be said to have exposed anything secret, it would probably be best characterized as bringing attention to 'public secrets': matters that were known to some but not explicitly acknowledged.[44]

What was clear was that the frequent admissions of a basic lack of knowledge or action had not compelled government officials to cast doubt on Her Majesty's Government's adherence to IHL. Ministers spoke one day to the stark lack of knowledge and on another with assurance about the scale of the humanitarian effects.[45] Neither logic nor parliament nor the media compelled government officials to speak consistently.

The deficiencies in the understanding of the US and UK did not just call into question what these specific governments knew, but what any governments could have known. If these major users were not gathering evidence from their combat experiences, then others would be unlikely to possess any such evidence either. Instead they would be reliant on assessments made by NGOs and inter-governmental agencies; assessments of the kind the US, UK, Israel, Russia, and others frequently criticized.[46]

Certainly prior to 2007 though, it would be difficult to find examples of states overtly challenging the basis of other states' claims, or even openly inquiring into what other states knew. As is too often the case, being diplomatic in this forum meant abiding by principles that were tantamount to collusion.[47] *Out of Balance* ended by arguing that these deficiencies meant the CCW:

is at risk of becoming a forum of empty overtures and political posturing that does not provide a credible process for developing IHL ... The overarching goal of states concerned with humanitarian problems of cluster munitions must be to ensure that IHL is used as a mechanism for the appropriate protection of civilians rather than as a fig leaf for belligerents. Within international legal fora such as the CCW, states that simply sit quiet in the face of incoherent arguments and inadequate evidence are failing vulnerable civilian populations now and in the future.[48]

ORDERS OF LEGITIMACY

In their examination of state crimes, Green and Ward proposed that 'a state is legitimate to the extent that: 1) it acts in accordance with the rules that it sets for itself and its citizenry; and 2) those rules are seen to be justified by shared beliefs'.[49] Jochnick and Normand adopted a similar two-pronged approach to legitimacy as part of arguing that the law of wars have 'facilitated rather than restrained wartime violence'.[50] They contended that this has taken place by those laws: 1) validating acts of violence by designating them as 'lawful'; and, more subtly, 2) serving the ideological function of reinforcing the perception of shared international values and a moral obligation to the existing distribution of geopolitical power. The latter included the acceptance of war making as practiced by dominant nations.

The previous sections suggested IHL served another ideological function: that of reinforcing a perception that states are competent. With its abstract demand for balance and the ease by which its achievement could be declared, the law provided a language through which officials could present conflict as being undertaken by knowledgeable and measured bodies.

Certainly by 2006, it was the growing belief of myself and others that what was being obscured in the case of cluster munitions was not simply a bias in the way weighing was undertaken. Rather, what remained out of sight was a basic and fundamental lack of regard. The life and death consequences resulting from the use of cluster munitions were not being decided by a cold calculus of costs and benefits (however imperfectly performed), but rather by what appeared to be an institutional indifference. Again and again, the concerns identified by humanitarian-minded organizations were being dismissed through well-worn tropes.

As part of this, the suggestion that the 'balance' sought pertained to 'highly sensitive' situations where the public release of information 'could potentially cause significant harm [...] to troops on operations were it to fall into the wrong hands'[51] was taken as justification for sealing decision-making from outside scrutiny. This practice reached its logical but most dubious pinnacle in the UK where officials refused to indicate whether Her Majesty's Government had consulted its law officers on the legality of the use of cluster munitions.[52]

In other words, the legitimacy of conflict was based on what can be called a 'secretism': the 'active milling, polishing, and promotion of the reputation of secrets'.[53] Statements by government, about adhering to IHL, evoked a sense that much lay behind them: expertise, activities, care, preparations. Such evocations shored up the credibility of those speaking and those they spoke for.[54]

Some legal commentators acted in a manner complicit in this construction of states as competent. This was done, for instance, in positing that an unidentified someone, somewhere within the military-political establishment, was considering the 'whole picture'[55] of advantages and harms. Further, in their extensive use of hypothetical scenarios rather than concerning themselves with what was not known, certain legal analyses distracted attention from 'what had taken place' in favor of asking 'What if in scenario X a cluster munition were used in such and such an appropriate manner to...?'[56]

PUTTING IGNORANCE TO A TEST

The rest of this chapter describes a different orientation to evidence and argument. This one tested the ignorance of states, rather than being resigned to ignorance about ignorance.

In response to the inadequacies of the CCW, in February 2007 a Core Group[57] of governments initiated a series of multilateral conferences that sought to establish a binding treaty that would prohibit 'cluster munitions that cause unacceptable harm to civilians'. The US, China, India, and Russia were among those that did not join what became known as the 'Oslo Process'. The negotiations were assisted by the participation of groups from international civil society, most notably through the 400 plus organizations that make up the Cluster Munition Coalition (CMC).

On December 3, 2008, 94 states signed the Convention on Cluster Munitions (CCM). While allowing for certain exclusions, the CCM prohibits all those weapons commonly identified under this label that have been documented as causing significant humanitarian harms in the past or (as far as can be gauged) any civilian casualties.[58] The Convention came into effect on August 1, 2010.

A history of the Oslo Process and its relation to the CCW has been given elsewhere.[59] In this chapter the focus is on one aspect of what happened: how the definition of what counted as a 'cluster munition' was settled and, therefore, what should be banned. The Oslo Process started with a widely encompassing definition and then sought to determine what exclusions should be made to a ban. So rather than specifying what should be *prohibited,* the definition structure demanded that countries make a case for what exclusions should be *allowed.* As such, the presumption was that exclusions had to be 'argued in', rather than allowances 'argued out'.[60] This chapter develops the importance of this orientation in testing ignorance.

Consider these initial characterizations of the Oslo Process in contrast to one position advanced by the US. Against the expression of dissatisfaction with the CCW by many others, at one of its 2006 meetings the Head of the US delegation (Ronald Bettauer) reflected on his long history of engagement with cluster munitions. For him, the task at hand remained 'the same' over time:

> In 1974, I said: 'Our task is a humanitarian one – to find feasible restrictions for weapons shown to cause unnecessary suffering or to be indiscriminate in their effects. To accomplish this, we need sufficient information to permit us to make sound judgments. That does not mean exhaustive data is required, but rather that there must be a reasonably persuasive case. If we do not have such a case, we could end up making conflict less humane instead of more humane. To restrict a weapon not adequately shown to merit such restriction, may result in the use of weapons which could well lead to more suffering and less discrimination.'
>
> This remains true today, and it underlies my Government's approach. We have worked hard over the years to find the appropriate balance for humanitarian and military interests, to clarify the facts, and to seek consensus for appropriate restrictions on conventional weapons where that is warranted.[61]

The implication of Bettauer's statement was that even after 30 years a reasonably persuasive case had not yet been made for regulating – let alone banning – cluster munitions. What *would* count as a reasonably persuasive case was not elaborated, but the implication was clear: more evidence was required.

The Oslo Process followed a different logic. It combined the starting assumption that some cluster munitions 'cause unacceptable harm to civilians' with a definition structure that all weapons falling within the initial, broad understanding of cluster munitions were impermissible until the case was made otherwise. So, early on in the process Article 1 prohibited states from ever using, developing, acquiring, stockpiling, retaining or transferring cluster munitions. In Article 2, the definition was set out as:

> 'Cluster munition' means a munition that is designed to disperse or release explosive sub-munitions, and includes those explosive sub-munitions. It does not mean the following:
> (a) ...
> (b) ...
> (c) ...[62]

Exclusions were meant to be argued in as part of '(a) ... (b) ... (c) ...'. Instead of following the typical pattern in disarmament negotiations of making critics justify why specific weapons should be banned, the Oslo Process started with a wide-ranging ban and then put it to those arguing for exclusions to justify why anything within that definition did not cause 'unacceptable harm'. This was not based on a sense that the case had already been made against all cluster munitions with absolute certainty, but rather that history justified a starting orientation that presumed they were problematic.

Stated differently, the burden of proof was on those seeking to retain options. The case for a restriction had been established by past usage, the case for exclusions to a ban was the one that had to be made. This approach was consistent with acknowledging doubt or disagreement about the humanitarian effects of these weapons, but included a presumption about where this should lead.

A remarkable feature of the Oslo Process was how little a positive case was made. A number of governments who took part in its process – Japan, Germany, the UK, Spain, Finland, Switzerland, the Netherlands, and France[63] – time after time argued for a less wide-ranging treaty definition. Yet – with the exception of Germany's efforts to retain its so-called sensor-fused submunitions – these states offered almost no evidence or detailed arguments in support of such exclusions. If the governments in the Oslo Process had informed analyses supporting such positions, they were not aired. This lack of depth was in line with past contributions to the CCW and previous government proclamations. In other words, their actions were consistent with the appraisal of widespread institutional ignorance made in previous sections of this chapter.

Ironically, the government that perhaps did most to corroborate both the military utility and humanitarian harms of civilians was Norway – one of the members of the Core Group of the Oslo Process and arguably the most pivotal nation in securing a ban. A report by the Norwegian Defence Research Establishment in collaboration with Norwegian People's Aid, for instance, provided in-depth field and trial assessments of one submunition type (the M85) that some governments favored retaining. The argument was made in this report that the M85's self-destruct mechanism would not ensure acceptable post-conflict contamination. On the military side, Norway provided an analysis of the comparative utility of cluster munitions with alternatives.[64] This analysis offered one of the most detailed public elaborations of the military advantages of cluster munitions. States that were calling for 'less' during the Oslo Process simply had nothing comparable to either of these Norwegian studies.

While those wishing to retain cluster munitions were put on the back foot through the definition structure, those pressing for a wide encompassing definition had many advantages. Rather than having to set out an argument of their own to get weapon systems prohibited, such states could pick apart the proposals for 'less' made by Japan, Germany, the UK, Spain, Finland, Switzerland, France, and others.[65] So throughout the Oslo Process, Ghana, Indonesia, Cambodia, Botswana, Fiji, Guatemala, Zambia, Jamaica, Lebanon, the Cook Islands, and others pointed to the history of humanitarian problems with cluster munitions to argue that the case for proposed exclusions had not been sufficiently demonstrated. Without such a case, a ban should apply.

The importance of shifting the onus can be underscored by thinking counterfactually about what would have happened if the process had been structured along more conventional lines. If progressive governments, or the Cluster Munitions Coalition, had to prove why certain submunitions needed to be banned, then this would have laid a substantial burden with them. Especially for small states with limited resources or combat experience, marshaling credible information would have proven highly onerous. Also, history would suggest that major military nations would have had ample ready-made lines to hand about why certain weapon systems could be assumed to be acceptable: claims that would have evoked a sense that much lay behind them.

Table 3.1 summaries the contrast in orientations pointed to in this chapter for establishing the 'facts of the matter' regarding cluster munitions: 'ruling out' and 'ruling in'.[66] Generally speaking, within the traditional interpretation of IHL these weapons were legal until proven otherwise, whereas in the Oslo Process the working presumption was that they were politically unacceptable until proven otherwise.

Table 3.1   'Ruling out' and 'Ruling in'

	'Ruling out'	*'Ruling in'*
Basic logic	Determining what should be proscribed	Justifying what should be allowed
What needs to be argued for?	Restrictions to use	Exclusions from prohibition
Evidence	Hypotheticals central	History central
Concern	Legality	Acceptability
Role for existing IHL	IHL based	Political process informed but not bounded by IHL
Evaluative basis	Case by case	Pattern of effects over time
Limitations sought	Specific	Categorical

Within this latter orientation, those highlighting the humanitarian consequences of cluster munitions had novel argumentative resources at their disposal. It was not so much that the maneuvers of secretism were unmasked as empty, rather that their lure was neutralized by being made less germane because past tactics for deflecting criticism were no longer sufficient to carry the day. When pressed to speak to the sort of evidence that informed their previously confident assessments that a balance had been struck as required under IHL, governments fell silent.[67]

DOING IGNORANCE

At its heart, international humanitarian law proposes that a balance be struck between military demands and damage to civilians. That balance has provided the vocabulary for war-fighting nations to speak to their conduct in armed conflict. In relation to cluster munitions, against evidence of the human toll of these weapons, many users and stockpiler states spoke with confidence that IHL had been followed.

In line with previous chapters, this one has dwelt on the subtle and shifting relationship between knowledge–ignorance as well as disclosure–concealment. While Chapter 2 considered efforts by government officials to work towards a state of ignorance, this one has considered efforts to work towards understanding the ignorance of officials. That entailed efforts to expose what, in many respects, was already disclosed: that ministerial briefings, ambassador statements, and other assurances that a balance had been struck between humanity and military necessity were based on inadequate information. What was described was a testing. As argued, when those alarmed about the likely effects of cluster munitions moved away from the language of the IHL and balance, to one of patterns and presumptions, uncertainties and unknowns that once hindered action became a source of argumentative strength.

Part II
Dialogues

4
Covert Conversations and Public Secrets?: The Banning of Cluster Munitions

Previous chapters charted the bounds of political debate about major issues of controversy in recent years associated with organized state violence. In significant ways, those limits have resulted from individuals claiming to hold definitive facts in slippery situations.

In contrast, what has been sought in this book is a recognition of the complex ways in which in the understanding of events is produced by the movements between disclosure and concealment. Here, more information does not necessarily shed more light or promote a shared understanding. So the publication of certain previously secret intelligence assessments of WMD threats provided officials, pundits, and others with additional grounds for disagreeing about what was known. In relation to Iraqi civilian deaths, the release of some government correspondence was used to pose additional questions about how to make sense of what had happened (and what had not).

It follows from these points that the analysis of government secrecy and transparency needs to attend to the claims it advances. Just as with other commentaries, the arguments of this book can be questioned for how they conceal and reveal as well as how they foster knowledge and ignorance. This chapter asks how we can fashion positive possibilities of knowing and acting with such a recognition.

What follows is an abridged account of a conversation between the author (BR) and two others that took place between August 10 and 11, 2009.[1] The aim is two-fold: 1) to probe how the negotiation of a ban on cluster munitions was tied up with the strategic management of information; and 2) to ask how the analysis of those disarmament negotiations itself entails managed negotiation of information.

As background, since 2003 the international civil society campaign against cluster munitions has been led by the Cluster Munition Coalition (CMC), a grouping that now consists of over

400 organizations from 90 countries. At the time of writing, Richard Moyes (RM) was a co-chair of the CMC and was in charge of handling its position on the definitions during the Oslo Process. 'A.N. Other' (AO) has been a significant contributor to international campaigns. A few months after August 2009, 'Other' decided not to be identified in any subsequent publications out of a concern that some of the comments below might be misconstrued or not taken in the spirit in which they were intended.

*   *   *

BR: So, reactions please to the background paper I wrote? I thought we might just work through it for our conversations today and tomorrow.

RM: I thought it was good, entertaining too. Before we plunge into it, what's this really all for? What you have written is all about structures of argument. As a professional generator of material related to processes of argumentation I can see why you did that, but thinking about purpose, there is the question of what we want to achieve out of this.

AO: Self-aggrandizing?

[Laughter]

RM: Is that how you see it?

BR: I suppose for me it is about being able to give a sort of insiders' history to the ban given that the two of you figured so prominently in the process. It would be about trying to highlight some of the subtler issues at stake in attributing rights and wrongs to technology in conditions of secrecy...

RM: Hmm ...

BR: ... and an opportunity to talk about some of the more conceptual issues I am preoccupied by.

RM: Yeah, well for me, I am keen to think about how forms of analysis like this can have utility in future situations. Important issues get written out of a lot of histories. As a result, they are less relevant and insightful for individuals working through processes because they write out the uncertainties that are the lived experiences of these processes.

AO: That sounds good to me. I think the role of individuals is too often underplayed too. Even reading the article the two of you wrote in *Non-proliferation Review* about the burden of proof,[2] there is no acknowledgement of individuals and the tensions that went on, it's all about ideas and the structure of arguments.[3]

RM: Yes.

AO: Then there is the whole question of what can be known, and what maybe is not OK that it is known because it might be bad for us, the Convention, or the future meaning of it. Exploring those issues is important too.

Background

BR: About Richard's point about lessons, I suppose one of my long-running preoccupations has been whether it was possible to find ways of analytical and practical engagement not solely based on throwing facts around. Even if we ignore the way many facts have been in short supply because of things unknown or made unknown, they can't resolve disputes about what is acceptable about the use of force. So, I know both of you have heard me talk about this in terms of adopting a skeptical orientation. That is sort of encapsulated in shifting the question at hand away from 'What are the effects of cluster weapons?' to something like 'How is it known that cluster weapons have certain effects?'...[4]

So, in past years, almost all of diplomatic debate about cluster munitions was framed in terms of whether they fell foul of the rules of IHL. With that kind of quasi cost–benefit analysis states like the US and Russia used the abstract possibility that certain types of cluster munitions might be employed without disproportionate humanitarian costs to close down any talk of a prohibition.[5]

AO: I am with you on the importance of the past IHL framing, it meant that it was those concerned about cluster munitions that have to prove they caused excessive damage. This, along with the inaccessibility of strike sites, meant we as members of civil society often didn't have the evidence necessary, in the eyes of many, to offer definitive assessments, certainly not evidence to prove that however they were used, cluster munitions would almost always fall foul of IHL.

RM: I look back to that early IHL discussion as a real testament to the power of professional discourse to stifle people. I remember a meeting, let us say in 2005, when United Nations Development Programme wanted to call for a ban and some in the CMC, you can guess who, were arguing that you couldn't because it was not legally justified. I interjected that just because existing IHL didn't *require* a ban didn't mean there might not be other grounds for one. That was rejected, no doubt partly because I couldn't lay out what these other grounds were in relation to some pre-authorized discourse.

After that I got sucked into the IHL type of framing for a while. Partly, I think, this was because the people shouting 'ban cluster bombs' didn't engage at all with the IHL arguments. I think I rationalized this orientation by saying that the strengthening of IHL in general was perhaps more important than the specific issue of cluster munitions, and for this reason it was important to give states an opportunity to take action through existing institutions. Certainly for me, a lot of factors were at play in my own subservience to IHL despite seeing the problem straight away – institutional identities and personal insecurities for a start.

Ignorance and Humanitarian Effects

BR: I saw the *Out of Balance*[6] and *Failure to Protect*[7] reports that we did, Richard, as an effort to test our emerging assessment of the ignorance of states. By making explicit that the UK and others had done next to nothing to assess the humanitarian effects of its use of cluster munitions.

AO: And the US, you could say the same about what the US knows. They admitted they hadn't done any studies of humanitarian effects at a meeting with Ken,[8] me, and some others a couple of years ago. It was at a conference you didn't attend.

BR: Yeah, no, I heard about that. What I was saying was that I hoped bringing to the fore *how* what was known was known would provide the inspiration for a different kind of political engagement, deflating the grand and abstract claims made about the careful weighing done under IHL. My thinking being that since it was those making critical remarks that had to do the running under IHL to prove what was what, getting states to start justifying how they knew what they said they knew could improve the sterile, well, non-discussions that were happening.

[Pause]

I trust both of you will agree that what has been so amazing is that the attempt to promote a debate has brought such a paltry substantive response. Here, I mean, in relation to facts and arguments. One presumes someone in some Ministry of Defence has some understanding of the humanitarian and military issues associated with cluster munitions, certainly they publicly projected such an understanding. After having probed for years though, I am left with little sense as to who.

RM: Knowing how much states know means knowing that they do not know very much.

AO: Yes, I would agree with that. States that used clusters have not closely scrutinized the CMC's position and they just didn't have detailed arguments to support their upbeat claims. The way the Oslo Process structured the definition, we were able to put them on the back foot. I know, Brian, you said you wanted to talk about burden of proof later, so maybe we can get into that then.

BR: Well we are kinda getting out of order here, but we can talk about it now. For me, thinking about what you said before about the role of individuals, some of my starkest memories of the Oslo Process are about how the burden mattered in personal interactions. So, in the background paper I distributed for our chat, I wrote out part of that exchange at the Wellington Conference between Ambassador Don MacKay and a UK representative.

RM: I remember it.

BR: The UK was proposing some major exclusions to what should be prohibited, and let me read what Don said. He asked: 'If one is looking at exclusion based on less than a certain number of sub-munitions, is your proposal that it is based on this alone, and, again, looking at the broader parameters we need to fit this into, how would one argue, how would you argue that that does not cause unacceptable harm to civilians? And I realize that is asking a quite large question, but I am sure our colleague from the United Kingdom is more than up to deal with it and I pass the floor'.

AO: Oh yeah, I remember that too, the response went around and around.

BR: Yeah, yeah. I don't think you could say the UK spokesperson was 'up to it'. In the end he said it was a matter of judgment. True enough, but those calling for a less wide-ranging definition during the process were the ones having to justify their judgments.

RM: It goes a lot further than that. Those that wanted to enact a distinction between cluster munitions that cause 'acceptable harm' versus 'unacceptable harm' in order to retain their weapons did not get anywhere near to agreeing that or even specifying how they would make that distinction.

BR: Yes, I mean, at one level, how could they? There isn't some sort of easy equation for calculating that. I know IHL assumes some sort of balancing is always done, but, really, it isn't like there is an accepted scale for weighing civilian costs and military advantages. The point was that the problem of proving the balance was a problem with those wanting to put in exclusions.

RM: There was another aspect to the strategy with the burden of proof I want to get on the record, maybe one less visible. I argued consistently and I think persuasively that when the definition of cluster munitions was debated in Wellington and Dublin that the discussion start from the most sophisticated end of the technology spectrum, based on a sense that if governments couldn't argue those in, they would not be able to argue in lesser measures. And even if they were able to argue those more sophisticated technologies, the arguments they would have to use would undermine their claims that anything less should be exempted. So by controlling the structure of debate, even 'successful' arguments might actually serve to tighten the noose.

Definitions, Governments, and Secrecy

BR: So, [AO], how did that happen that the definition introduced into the process at Vienna had the starting presumption against cluster munitions? I was not party to the backstage negotiations with the government officials in the Oslo Process.

AO: Well, really it was touch and go. I would say that I was more worried about that than anything else at any time during the process.

RM: Well ...

AO: Honestly. Around the time leading up to Vienna I would say very, very few people, including in the Core Group of governments or the CMC leadership, grasped the importance of banning the whole category of cluster munitions. I had many email exchanges and telephone conversations, and I was really getting worried. While obviously a number of people came around later, at the time it wasn't like that. Markus from Austria knew though, he got it because of his experience with us and Judith and his own national law,[9] and if the conference hadn't been in Vienna with the Austrians chairing, I think we could easily have lost it.

BR: OK, well that is with the states advancing a prohibition. What about those within the Oslo Process but asking for less. Did those states simply not realize until it was too late the general advantages conferred by the definitional approach adopted? It just doesn't make sense to me that experienced officials would not see, and so oppose, this way of establishing the prohibition.

AO: Some did, just a few, some in the UK did – some did oppose it.

RM: Not really though.

AO: No they did, in Vienna, there was quite a bit of opposition.

RM: Sure, but never very organized and never very effective. I mean, if they would have opposed the definition structure at that time in anything like a concerted way, they could have gotten something else.

AO: Ah ...

RM: Of course, it is an open question of what any government is and what it really wanted out of this. We don't want to present states like the UK, Australia, or Japan as opposing any humanitarian movement at all. Since they took part in the Oslo Process and signed the treaty we have to assume they wanted to ban this category of weapons. Don't we?

[Pause]

RM: You're shaking your head.

[Pause]

RM: I just wonder whether we should maintain this sense that they didn't want to do it.[10] Maybe ministers wanted to do it but were prevented by the bureaucracy. So there is the question of what any country is, like the UK?

AO: The queen.

RM: We could consider the case of the Dutch that originally funded the CMC. They got it off the ground. What can we infer from a state in the process of resisting a comprehensive ban being the one that also funded the establishment of the civil society group leading international criticism?

AO: No that's right. We as NGOs were often trying to help one part of a government against another too, so typically working with ministries of foreign affairs against their defense colleagues. If it hadn't been for people in key departments sticking their head above the parapet to take risks, we would have never had the treaty. If officials hadn't gone against their policy lines in private conversations to be helpful to us, forget it. ▇▇▇▇▇▇▇ summed it up nicely at that *Banning Cluster Munitions* report[11] launch when he said, what was it? Something like 'Obviously we do not mention the work of many government officials in this report, partly because if we did mention you, you would get sacked'.

BR: Wow.

AO: And he said it in front of all of the government people at a public meeting. It was an open recognition that this process was substantially achieved because a lot of individuals worked against their own governments' position.

BR: The making of a public secret.

RM: I thought it was great. A sense to governments that the process worked by us turning their agents against them – and that we all secretly knew this.

AO: Supreme confidence.

RM: It pushed at a boundary that I did not think would be acceptable.

AO: I liked it because it got out a message that people need to take personal responsibility beyond their institutions. So change happens when people step beyond their mandate.

BR: Well, there's an interesting dynamic at work there in revealing a public secret. I mean, it would have been extremely unlikely that after ▇▇▇▇▇▇ said that anyone would stand up and say that was not the case, that that never happened at anytime. How could anyone say what happened behind the scenes in events they were not involved in? They would have been putting themselves in the hot-seat in terms of needing to say more. The exposure of secrets is often resistant to questioning like this. And because of that lack of likely challenge, ▇▇▇▇▇▇ could build up a sense of collective identity and define what 'really' happened in the process.

RM: Back to the matter of what states wanted though, it's actually quite complicated because I think there were also people saying things to us that appeared, on the surface, to be false. I remember ▇▇▇▇▇▇ took aside my old boss very early on in this process and said 'we are on your side'. Well, it is very difficult to see how. Certainly one thing I don't know but I want to know is how the process and its outcomes were represented within certain governments, especially to ministers.

AO: There has been a lack of honesty in terms of positions, well, patent dishonesty in some cases. Governments talking about humanitarian imperatives, when they should have been talking about state control and sovereignty. If you look at many of the proposals offered for what should be banned over the last few years, they were not drawn around arguments based on information from testing regimes or some sense of how to gauge humanitarian harms, but rather on what existing stockpiles a country had. They were coming up with proposals to keep what they had. Period.

Strategic Disclosure and Concealment

BR: On the matter of the lack of engagement and strategy by some states, I don't know what is going to come out of our discussions in terms of a product, but I am wondering whether either of you would have any qualms about what got told as part of that. So, do you think that might matter for the future? I mean, do you think that some sort of all-chips-on-the-table revelation, whatever that might be, would jeopardize attempts to secure prohibitions in the future?

RM: Despite what I said about a goal of this for me being sharing lessons learned, sometimes I think you could write it all down and in the future people would not see it. Partly because I think states often had to delude themselves. During a process like this, diplomats have to tell their ministers that everything is under control. They cannot say they are on a slippery slope to losing everything. And now afterwards those very officials that were arguing for a weaker treaty are offering glowing internal briefs about the CCM. I just can't see how, in these conditions, bureaucracies can learn lessons all that effectively.

AO: Also, I think that those opposing humanitarian initiatives would discount our analysis. My personal sense is that the officials of certain states, mainly those outside the process, were, well, too arrogant. Though that might sound arrogant of me to say it. Maybe dismissive is the right word. They thought they would not be beaten by a coalition of NGOs and middle-power states ...

RM: ... Again. Simon Conway and I sat in a meeting with UK FCO officials, probably in 2005, and they said directly: 'don't think you will get away with doing on cluster munitions what was done on landmines'.

AO: And I think that this goes for states outside the Oslo Process like the US. If they do an after-action report on the process, they should recognize that they should've engaged more.

RM: In many respects I was extremely open with the UK government about our strategy.

AO: I was actually worried about the level of your strategic sharing.

RM: Yeah, I gave them suggestions about how I would have argued the case for retaining cluster munitions if I was in their shoes.

BR: Why?

RM: It's a good question. I guess it was a matter of confidence. You can feel in yourself that you are being completely honest if you can give people your best assessment of how the arguments could play out. You don't need to feel like you are holding back lines of argument, that you are going to trump them with in a sort of 'I beat you' way. You are framing it quite differently. You are framing it in terms of 'here is what I am thinking, here are my arguments'. It is not oppositional, it is about mutual problem-solving. Though, clearly, at other times I framed things in very oppositional terms.

BR: But what if they came back with one of your arguments?

RM: We would've had to come up with better arguments. It is not like any argument does not have a counter-argument.

AO: And there were little traps.

RM: Yeah, in the sense that what I gave them would have also bought them into larger framings about the need for precautionary principle-type approaches or the importance of area effects. That sort of thing. So even if they had used those arguments, then we would have them extending themselves in ways we wanted.

BR: Umm ...

RM: I didn't see what needed doing through this process as just banning whatever stuff could be banned, but rather putting in place something tactical that could be built on in the future. And operating more in terms of mutual problem-solving and mutual examination of the different underpinning viewpoints is itself part of taking much of the battleground, because, what do they do? They can either step on to your terrain and start engaging in that discussion or they don't, and they have that disengagement noticed.

AO: Thinking about the issue of what we disclose, I guess you have to have a sense of balance between openness and disclosure in terms of how it can be used for or against progressive change.

RM: That is a fundamental issue about knowledge and how it is handled, and my sense would be that you err on the side of disclosure, basically. I think that sets the right tone. We just have to be confident in that position. Having said that, I can think of ways states could have avoided getting trapped in the CCM that I am not sure I would want shared.

AO: Besides matters of personalities clashing, quite a number actually, I would be uncomfortable openly discussing certain things like ...

BR: ... Certain states' policy positions being written by the CMC?

AO: ... the way NGO activists can create the space for those within risk-adverse bureaucracies. There were so many instances in which officials said to us quietly to please hit their governments in the media so that they could move it forward. They wanted and worked for their governments to look out of touch, ignorant, uncaring, unengaged. I'm not sure how much I want to get into that.

BR: If we look at the Oslo Process, then it certainly strikes me as plausible to argue that states have been able to shore up their image of being responsive to humanitarian concerns because of what has not been said.

AO: Such as?

BR: Well, I may have missed something, but I don't remember many suggestions being aired publicly that governments have been acting in bad faith in the past. Some because they were making unsubstantiated claims for years, if not decades, about cluster munitions. Others because they have been complicit in not offering criticisms.

RM: The failings of the international community are systematic ...

BR: Sure, and in the informal banter we have joked about this, but the way things were presented in public forums bought into an image of the international community consisting of responsible and responsive states. Is this too abstract to be a concern? For reasons I can't articulate, this really worries me.

RM: No, that's right. The nation state reaffirmed itself as the most appropriate framework for the management and undertaking of violence, parading this latest commitment to do better in the future as a badge of accountability!

AO: Linking up to what I said before, there has been little critical attention to the concept of expertise. I mean, a lot of states came to us during the process to ask what we thought. I am glad if they did this rather than going to France or Germany, say, but still, I felt unless we gave them a clear steer on the options that people might swing on to a very different position because of some fantasy concern. I felt awkward because people were definitely putting a trust in me as a NGO person to give an objective account.

BR: This was like with the Spanish proposal at Dublin for exclusions that favored its stockpiles.

RM: Yeah, sure, some Latin countries really seemed to go for its proposal because, it would seem, because Spain is Spanish speaking ... Suddenly, if you read the diplomatic records, it feels like Spanish-speaking countries are repeating the exclusions Spain proposed.[12]

AO: It was a smart move.

RM: Yeah, but there we were about to lose a broad coalition because not that many states seemed to see the implications of what was being said. Their position came down to something else. Something like, I don't know, that they could easily converse with another government about technical matters. On the other side, you had states not just arguing that cluster munitions were unacceptable, but that all weapons were. In a process set up to single out one group of technology from others, those sorts of statements were not necessarily that helpful.

Ignorance, Burdens, and Advocacy

BR: So we have been talking a lot about states. I wonder if we could turn to NGOs and the CMC. Thinking about who knew what, how many people actively weighed in on the matter of definitions in any detail before Dublin? Several? That figure would be within the right order of magnitude based of my experience. How many people considered the logic of the definition in relation to other possibilities and bought into its logic before then? I do not know, I am just asking. I have spoken with a number of campaigners throughout the Oslo Process and the overwhelming impression I get is that the answer would be 'not many'.

AO: Yeah, I don't know how far to push this, the way the matter of definitions, like other topics, was handled by a handful of people in the CMC steering group. So there is a way in which you could talk about the construction of ignorance within the CMC itself. So the split between those campaigners pressing for an all out ban and those people setting the policy that had a sense of the need for some exclusions that were not problematic.

RM: What we didn't do enough was to take our analysis to the CMC and ask them what they thought. We basically decided we were the people that knew what we should think.

AO: Others were busy with other things too. They just did not have time during much of the last few years. That did change.

BR: The reason I am asking is that the potential for the CCM to set precedents and new standards for the future might be limited because of the lack of discussion about the definition of what got banned. So, if I can put it this way, you guys didn't make the definition structure a big issue because you were trying to sneak it into the treaty.

RM: On the quiet.

BR: Yeah, because you didn't want states to react against it. And now, because we are in the process of ratification,[13] you still don't want to be too loud about the wider advantages we see in the CCM because it might put some states off.

AO: Yeah.

BR: I am concerned about that because I read from some progressive people an attempt to fit the treaty into an IHL framing that I think fails to acknowledge how the convention went beyond the past failings of IHL[14] ...

Just thinking about it now though, I wonder whether the reversing of the burden of proof structure was associated with certain negative consequences. So the basic CMC message to campaigners and states was to question the adequacy of arguments put forward by states wishing to retain cluster weapons. But if you just suggest people counter the claims of others, they do not necessarily have to get stuck into the details themselves. Might that have meant people were sort of disempowered of the issues at hand?

RM: I don't like the word disempowering, but I agree the skeptical countering approach enshrined a degree of disengagement among CMC campaigners and some states. When it got tense at the end in Dublin, I didn't think that many had a sense of how we got to that point. A number of us had to work quite a bit to get to that situation in Dublin to be faced with the dilemmas and choices we were faced with there. Because I don't think many people saw that, the understandings within the CMC and with some states were fragile. There are still underlying questions in my mind about to what extent, in the end, we did give in to industry and compromised about the exclusions to the definition in order to get certain states to sign the treaty – but they don't keep me awake at night.

AO: The final text is a compromise in my mind, obviously because it's a negotiation and you can't expect to get 100 percent of what you want, but we came pretty close. On the original point though, if people wanted to get engaged in a detailed way with the issues, they could have. It was hardly necessary that the reverse burden of proof and the way the definition was set necessitated some sort of deficiency in understanding or engagement.

RM: There were states though whose basic interventions throughout the process were to say that what others said wasn't good enough. I don't think you could argue that all of them had a great grasp of the finer details.

AO: Yes, but the scope was there for people to use that framework to get engaged with the issues if they wanted to. And we did reach out a lot, particularly before Dublin both with campaigners and with governments. That was one of the CMC's key goals from the regional conferences before Dublin. I thought we were quite systematic about it.

Censorship, Absences, and Inquiry

RM: One of the things I would like to know is what were the strategies and plans people devised, in NGOs and governments, that just never came out in the process, because they weren't required, because someone above them told them 'no', because people were unsure of themselves, or whatever.

BR: So on unknowns. Just thinking about whatever comes out by way of a product of our conversation, I suppose the question could be asked of it, 'Well you guys are not giving a full account of the Oslo Process and even in relation to the topics you do mentioned you are leaving out information, so what's the use of this history?'.

AO: Who is to say we are not going to be open? What I'd say is have a first go at writing up this dialogue and then send it to us for comments and see if we object. We can delete what we are uncomfortable sharing. We might not delete anything.

BR: One of the things I would like to do is to acknowledge the things that have been said in our conversation but that are not being included in the write-up of it. Because within typical academic accounts, readers rarely know that there are things that are not being included.

AO: So you want to write in the conversation that I am saying that there are things that shouldn't be repeated.

RM: You should write in that we are erring on the side of keeping things in and you, as an academic, are saying 'No, we have to take them out.'

[Laughter]

BR: I will put in you said that.

RM: So that is part of the point, to signpost what is absent from other accounts and, indeed, from that future account of us as well.

BR: Yeah.

RM: And also, it is going to talk about ignorance and absence in the process. This for me is very important in terms of, well, hopefully empowering people in future, empowering them in relation to the notion of uncertainty and ignorance because standardized histories tend to write this out because they have a narrative structure that makes you feel you are moving inevitably from the beginning to the end. I can't think of anything like this for the Mine Ban Treaty. That sort of history of experience and ideas.

BR: No, that's right. I think we are especially able to talk about uncertainties because we are not trying to look back with hindsight at what happened years ago.

RM: For me, anything that shows the level of doubt involved is a way of owning the problems associated with that doubt. It is a matter of getting on the front foot. I want to be there first and saying that there are gaps here and then framing those. I think it is about being open to risk and owning those risks through being open.

AO: I think it is important to acknowledge that our conversation has not just started. Since 2004 we have tried to follow certain principles, debating what needs to be done. So let's highlight those to see how they have been of benefit to others.

BR: Well, yeah, the only reason I can have this sort of frank exchange with you two is that we have known each other for years.

AO: True. Academics and students come and ask me what happened in the process and I don't really get into any of this. Partially because they don't ask the right questions and partially, I don't know, I just don't.

BR: What isn't in social research is becoming a pervasive concern for me. Academic types can't really just think of research as opening the curtains to let the light shine. Maybe that is a good analogy at points, but things are often far more complicated than that. What we focus on can create blind spots elsewhere, there are always alternative ways of describing things, making some people aware of something has implications for those not made aware, etc.

RM: I suppose I would see that at a kinda moral level. We talked before, Brian, about moving away from an 'us and them' framing. We have been having a bash at some states so far. Clearly governments have withheld information from the populations they serve. But if I have to be honest, NGOs are selective as well. I don't think the two are equivalent, but we can't simply pat ourselves on the back for being such good guys.

AO: It raises an important issue because the quality and the rigor of NGO use of data is one of the few ways our legitimacy as institutions can be assessed.

BR: For me there are representational issues here too. I suppose I'm thinking about to what extent it is possible to devise modes of representation that sensitize about how ignorances and uncertainties figure within social relations and how they help constitute claims to knowledge about those relations.

RM: But there are going to be limits to that.

BR: Huh.

RM: Are you going to put the swearing in? It's a question isn't it, about language and representation. Is the swearing not appropriate for academic things?

[Laughter]

BR: Who is to say I will not be open?

AO: But, it would make us sound less intelligent, less credible, authoritative.

[Laughter]

BR: Well, yeah, there is no escape from the tensions of representation just because you choose one form of writing. I'd prefer to keep the tensions in. We want to talk about unknowns, ignorance, and duplicity. Well it is always going to be a tension-ridden affair to give a presence to what is missing in some way. I'll think about what that means for swearing.

AO: If you are talking about writing conventions, I don't know enough about, the bloody standard literature you are supposing this would be a contribution towards in order to understand why this would be a good format. I'm kinda in the dark.

RM: Well let's keep ...

BR: ... Let's keep ███████ in the dark.

[Laughter]

[Discussion continues]

COMMENTARY

As a supplement to the previous chapter, this one provided a discussion of how the definition for a 'cluster munition' was settled within the agreement of the Convention on Cluster Munitions. That negotiation sought to question what lay beyond the confident assertions some officials publicly trumpeted, but simultaneously shielded from scrutiny.

As contended, the story of recent international efforts to ban cluster munitions is one that cannot be told without attending to how information was strategically exchanged. While governments and members of civil society notionally occupied distinct roles and often held oppositional positions, in practice such distinctions were blurred. Backstage officials and campaigners shared (at least some) information and strategies as part of attempts to achieve shared agendas.[15] It was also known, by many taking part in negotiations, that functionaries acted with campaigners to make their governments appear culpable. The transgression of telling the 'public secrets' associated with the extent of that joint action marked the bounds of what was commonly overtly acknowledged.

Another limit was the extent of critique regarding the political accountability of individual nations and the international community. As a (generally polite) political process organized by states (many of which were longstanding stockpilers or users of cluster munitions), governments were publicly treated as competent, trustworthy, and reasonable negotiators. This happened despite the unfounded claims given by some nations for years or the private reservations held about the motivations of certain officials. As a result, the political struggle that securing a ban on cluster munitions entailed, needs to be thought of in far more subtle terms than an exercise in unmasking or confronting.[16]

And yet, in seeking to recount such movements of concealment and revelation in international diplomacy, this chapter has engaged in the 'art of flirtation'[17] that is secret-telling. A form of writing was sought that sensitized readers to how absences figure within debates about social problems and the study of those debates, as well as how ignorance is born out of secrecy. The redactions, deletions, and allusions given have suggested various limits to disclosure, as well as disclosure about the limits of disclosure. With its ink scratchings, indirections have been placed, holes dug, holes partially filled, and inexpressibles expressed.

An underlying assumption of this chapter has been that in trying to report about issues where question marks exist about candor and openness, an account that does not direct attention to its own limitations should raise questions about how it was stitched together. An analysis that smoothes out such roughness denies the conditions under which it takes place and, presumably therefore, many of the reasons why it takes place. In acknowledgement of the uneasy conditions of secrecy, this chapter has asked how investigators can fashion alterative possibilities for telling. A telling of secrets has been given here, but one that recognizes its own incompleteness. In doing so, an appreciation has been sought of how ignorance is produced through the claim-making of officials, campaigners, and academics.[18]

With the flagging of the contingencies of what has been disclosed, the dialogue could be interpreted as an instance of an attempt to induce ignorance and an effort to work against it. Ignorance was fostered because details were withheld that are necessary for establishing the significance and meaning of what was written.[19] And yet, the explicit and implied recognition of the bounds of disclosure itself helped acknowledge a 'meta-ignorance'[20] about knowing what was not made known.[21]

Rather than just acknowledging how it entailed secret-keeping, this chapter has sought to turn incompleteness into a resource. With its play of revelation and concealment, the conversational writing format is meant to epitomize the negotiation of revelation and concealment prevalent in international diplomacy. An experimental form of writing has been taken to convey an 'experiential appreciation'[22] of what it is like to undertake inquiry in conditions of managed disclosure. That has meant highlighting the tensions, uncertainties, and contradictions associated with knowing and conveying matters that cannot be wholly known or conveyed. In other words, rather than just evaluating how information is strategically managed (as in Chapter 3), this chapter has sought to show this. If readers are left wondering what has been left out of the conversation in this chapter, this parallels the experiences of those engaged in international diplomacy.

My hope as an author therefore is not that readers attempt to decipher what was written to unlock its real meaning, but instead that the dialogue encourages what this book seeks to foster: an agile mindfulness of how revelation and concealment mix and meld.

5
Binding Options

Previous chapters examined the depiction and defense of state violence. Attempts to legitimate it took place as part of unfolding moves of political partisanship, claim and counter claim about military necessity, struggles for democratic control of public bodies, and persistent disputes about the meaning of rules. Disagreement has been evident in relation to what should count as 'the facts', whether they had been established, their importance, and what follows from them.

Doubt has also figured centrally in previous chapters. Reasons have been presented for disbelieving governments' aspirations to minimize humanitarian harms. Reasons have also been given for doubt regarding the scrutiny given by those entrusted with policing the state: political representatives, the media, official inquiries, and so on. As a result, it is not simply that those examining statecraft are faced with a choice regarding whether they seek to understand or change it. Understanding often requires active intervention that disturbs the status quo.

Further complicating doubt though, with the haunting allure that often characterizes state secrets, knowing what is known can be highly problematic. The topics examined suggested that much effort can be required to make the hidden visible, as well as the ways the visible hides. Repeated concerns were voiced about the dangers associated with mistaking what has been exposed and captured. These have not just stemmed from restrictions placed on access to information. Misgivings have been raised about buying into a logic of unmasking. So while ignoring ignorance gaps might not be helpful, striving to 'fill' them brings its own grounds for caution.

Investigating the intersection of the state and violence then is tension ridden. Active intervention and the questioning of what is known seem well justified. But knowing how to intervene or what to question are not so straightforward.

This chapter sets out a number of forward-looking options for challenging statecraft. Following on from the prior chapter, rather than specifying definitive prescriptions for thought and action, what is sought here is to cultivate a mindfulness of how to go on with our challenges to violence while questioning what it is we are doing. The options discussed are envisioned as cycles of reflection, planning, and action into what we know as well as how we know what we know.

As part of this chapter, what counts as better or worse by the way of direction will itself need to be questioned. A starting assumption is that much scope for disagreement and doubt is possible with regard to devising strategies for inquiry. Opposing arguments can be given about the wisdom of any proposal. This is not least because interventions can generate reactions that produce undesirable and unexpected outcomes. Acknowledging such difficulties associated with determining what to do though, is not taken as posing an insurmountable barrier to any action. Instead, in this chapter it is taken as a precondition for considered strategy. Inconsistencies, inversions, and dilemmas will be raised with a view to their binds as well as their inspirations.

DEMANDING TRANSPARENCY

Consider then such forked implications in relation to efforts to improve transparency. In relation to the shadowy crevices of statecraft, calls for exposing matters to the light are routine. Particularly for consequential and controversial matters such as the use of force, openness is often seen as fundamental to ensuring accountability. Transparency is needed to ensure that publics can assess the justifications given for actions taken on their behalf. The failure to provide necessary information then undermines the substantive legitimacy of the state.[1]

As noted in the Introduction though, transparency should not be treated as unproblematic. Clarifying sight in one direction can obscure in others. Further grounds for caution were raised in subsequent chapters. The official inquiries into WMD claims in Chapter 1 illustrated the shifting refractions of light meant to produce transparency. However, specifying what sort of openness was achieved by the varied inquiries examined would not be a simple task.

Moreover, despite the many investigations that placed an unpredicted amount of material into the public domain, the debate about spin and WMD was replete with what was still not opened up. As in the cases of Lord Butler's defense of his inquiry's conclusions, or in efforts by critics to pin blame on former British Prime Minister

Tony Blair, the absent functioned as an open-ended resource for making claims about truth and meaning. What pieces of the puzzle were deemed missing decreased or increased depending on who was arguing what and when. The potential for appealing to what was not disclosed is always possible and often proves potent.

While it is certainly imaginable that wide-ranging agreement can be reached about what happened without some absolute 'full disclosure', previous chapters have also indicated how such agreement is often frustrated. Following on from this, transparency is not so much a condition to be achieved as a complex set of practices, expectations, and ideals. Therefore, it is important to ask what is sought from its demand.

Previous chapters have indicated both the potential and the frustrations of transparency. In relation to the lack of assessment about the humanitarian effects of cluster munitions, Chapter 3 outlined how the long history of (modest) levels of disclosure enabled government duplicity and, as a result, for underpinning a rethinking of critique. Yet, as argued in Chapter 2, that strategy of identifying contradictions between official statements and practice is often tricky. One problem is ambiguity. Officials can – and often do (whether they intend it or not) – employ terms such as 'reliable' in ways that potentially support a range of stances regarding what was meant by what was said. The resulting wiggle-room can provide the space to deny the necessity of action or to facilitate a break with the past without any acknowledgement that this is being done.

Another danger of leveraging statements against each other is that this can result in a tightening down of communication. So, efforts to achieve greater transparency to outsiders can lead to a 'politics of consistency'[2] inside. Bureaucratic organizations, such as government ministries, can use this appearance of consistency as a sign of the soundness of their policies. So, for instance, Chapter 2 drew extensively on Freedom of Information (FoI) requests to contrast the front-stage of political statements about Iraqi deaths with the backstage of ministerial responses, to estimations produced by others. Page 46 refers to a December 2007 correspondence about a public service agreement regarding conflict prevention and resolution. In relation to attempts to devise measures for gauging conflict, as part of that exchange one British Foreign Office official responded:

There is intense FOI and parliamentary interest in [Iraqi civilian deaths] – if we started using figures internally now as a measurement of progress, we would risk having to release them under an FOI request, which would contradict previous statements that we do not collate or endorse any casualty figures.[3]

If it is correct to read the excerpt above as indicating that the fear of being seen to change positions was reason for reluctance in contributing to emerging policy initiatives aimed at measuring the harms of conflict, then this should give pause to how positive change can be secured. At once, this passage encapsulates many of the complexities associated with openness: how what is concealed (this inter-ministerial correspondence in the past) can be revealed through greater transparency measures (the establishment of FoI systems) as well as how efforts to reveal can end up stifling disclosure.

When those of us who seek to reduce the humanitarian consequences of conflict approach transparency, we need to do so with a recognition of its many facets: it is often seen as a something valuable in itself, a currency in contests of authority and legitimacy, and a fraught accomplishment. Attempts to open up do not so much expose the raw truth as set the basis for further contests and questions about what is known and how this is so.[4]

ESTABLISHING THE FACTS

Calls for transparency are often made as part of attempts to determine the facts of what happened. As indicated in past chapters, through gaining access to information that was otherwise out of bounds, much effort has been directed at proving the actual number of civilian deaths or establishing whether intelligence was really politicized. In contrast, I have sought to ask about the processes and conditions whereby facts get established as a way of mapping the boundaries and blind spots of debate.

Both approaches – settling what happened and setting out how debate unfolded – rely on assumptions about what counts as relevant and important information. Yet what is sought from the 'facts' differs across the two. What has been advocated in this book is a process of transformative inquiry rather than an attempt to find and fix down enduring truths. What has been sought are cycles of reflection and intervention that lead to the generation of new understandings, that can then open up new questions and possibilities that, in turn, lead to subsequent reflection and intervention.

Consider these points in relation to ongoing efforts to estimate deaths from armed violence. In recent years, some governments, inter-governmental organizations, and others have argued that armed violence poses a major impediment to development. They have also gone a step further by agreeing to work towards its reduction.[5] In 2006, for instance, the *Geneva Declaration on Armed Violence and Development* was launched. Among other goals, the 100-plus nations in the *Declaration* have committed themselves to 'achieve, by 2015, measurable decreases in the global burden of armed violence and tangible improvements in human security worldwide.'[6]

With these initiatives, the need to gather evidence and devise means of measurement has been a central priority. Producing such data is the very stuff of politics. Under the armed violence agenda, governments have been asked to undertake basic steps that many have proven uninterested, unwilling or unable to undertake in the past. For instance, in April 2011, 15 humanitarian and human rights NGOs called on those engaged in the conflict in Libya to record all civilian casualties.[7] With the linking of armed violence and development, this evidence-gathering extends far beyond the typically narrow range of consequences given attention.

Whatever the progressive mandate of such efforts, attempts to establish the facts of armed violence in order to guide policy are likely to be fraught. A limitation of the state-level international armed-violence agenda to improve surveillance and data-gathering capacity is that it is largely directed at developing countries.[8] Yet, previous chapters have given reasons for why any deficiencies should not be leveled there alone. For all their apparent sophistication, governments such as the US and the UK have not undertaken or supported data collection in many conflicts, let alone used the information gathered in some purposeful fashion.

The 2011 NATO air campaign in Libya was the latest example.[9] Although it appears that NATO forces only employed precision guided munitions, reports and NGOs working on the ground in Libya found evidence of scores of deaths from aerial strikes.[10] Despite its mandate to protect civilians, NATO first repeatedly denied these killings, and then failed to properly investigate them, provide compensate for civilian deaths, or to release vital information about the strikes in question to the UN.[11] As a result of such a pattern of practice, a crucial dimension for assessing international efforts to gauge violence will be how they affect the practices of major industrialized nations.[12] Certainly the US and the UK should not be accepted as standard bearers for others.

A second fraught aspect of establishing the facts of violence is that the contribution of measurements in making suffering recognizable is complex and debatable. As seems clear, from the intense efforts in the US and elsewhere to monitor the exact number of their troops killed and injured in recent conflicts, that counts are treated as a meaningful way of – however inadequately and incompletely – acknowledging loss. Furthermore, numbers at least offer the possibility of signifying individual suffering – something often denied in the rhetorics of war.[13] And yet, as bureaucratic tabulating exercises, casualty statistics provide a summation of abstractions that stifle comprehension as they enable it. Casualty numbers on their own cannot determine how those numbers should be understood – whether they are disproportionate, relatively small, a cost that needed to be paid, and so on.

As a third danger, such high-level government initiatives designed to improve data-gathering capacity and international standards could become insular technocratic exercises. As has been argued in relation to global warming research, attention to narrow technical issues of the comparative strength of methodologies and indicators can displace addressing who needs to do what.[14] In relation to determining deaths from conflict, it does not require too much imagination to envision how this could take place in relation to the armed violence agenda.

For instance, within popular and scholarly circles in Western countries since 2003, much debate has taken place about the relative merits of methodologies for assessing civilian deaths from conflict, the appropriateness of their assumptions, and the reasons for statistical uncertainty.[15] Proponents of alternative methodologies have forwarded (their own) approaches in order to authoritatively end dispute.[16] As in Chapter 2, government officials have pointed to such disputes as a way of suggesting that it is not possible to 'reliably' establish deaths. In the future, claims of 'unknowability' and endless calls for 'further research' could block practical efforts to reduce the burden of armed violence.

A fundamental limitation of trying to establish 'the facts' is that more is at stake than simple technical disputes about how to count. Instead, the basic question must be addressed regarding what lives should be counted. Should, for instance, only deaths from violence to civilians be measured? What about indirect deaths due to the loss of sanitation or medical facilities or normal daily routines? What about those deaths when it is not clear if it is a civilian or a combatant? What about those who would have been born save for their parents being killed?[17] The response given to such 'methodological' questions are inexorably tied to how the object of conflict is defined.

Each of the attempts to calculate the figures mentioned in Chapter 2 made different starting assumptions about what deaths to measure, something routinely not even acknowledged in many popular commentaries on Iraqi deaths.[18] Academic analysis has furthered the promotion of ignorance by taking on board the terms of these commentaries in order to make wider claims about the politics of statistics.[19] When Wikileaks released the US war logs that related to direct Iraqi deaths in October 2010, this was another occasion for more or less notice being taken of what had been counted.[20] This lack of recognition raises the specter that it is not just ambiguity that characterized the public discussion of Iraqi dead. Instead, there may have been a fundamental lack of joint understanding about what was being discussed – what Best referred to as 'inter-subjective ambiguity'.[21]

Without attention to the matters raised above, assessments of armed violence could well become sterile or, certainly at least, less skillful than they would be otherwise. Take, for instance, the *Charter for the Recognition of Every Casualty of Armed Conflict.* Launched in the early autumn of 2011 by the Every Casualty Program of the Oxford Research Group, the Charter called for 'resolute action by states to ensure that every direct casualty of armed conflict is: promptly recorded, correctly identified, and publicly acknowledged'.[22] In making these demands, its nearly 40 NGO signatories were demanding a radical transformation of current state practice.

Such an initiative does not just involve technical questions about how to collect and verify data. In many respects, these are secondary to the central consideration of what should be counted in the first place. In casting attention to *direct* casualties, only a subset (and often times a small subset) of deaths would be captured by the Charter's recoding calls – no matter how exhaustively carried out. While Chapter 2 indicated concerns with the way 'reliable' figures were made unknowable, to go in the other direction and argue that some definitive figure can be established brings its own hazards. Instead, the practical and specific purposes sought from figures need to be recognized.

Counts could serve many purposes: monitoring the use of force, memorializing suffering, determining assistance requirements, assessing the extent of criminal behavior, and acknowledging those departed. For some purposes and in some situations, attending to only direct deaths might be appropriate. Yet just what purpose should be sought and what sort of situation is transpiring are contestable. Ultimately, the question of what deaths should be counted is one that calls for deliberation rather than simple thoroughness. If the *Charter for the Recognition of Every Casualty of Armed Conflict* or other such initiatives were to contribute to a certain number being taken as literally 'every casualty' to a conflict, this would be regrettable. Such an abstraction would be gained at the expense of losing sight of the purpose served for figures. Following from the analysis of political and media coverage in Chapter 2, it is easily foreseeable how failing to acknowledge the purposes sought and the types of casualties recorded would not 'enable more timely, transparent, reliable, and comprehensive monitoring of armed violence than has been achieved before',[23] but instead weaken accountability.

In short, attempts to determine the humanitarian effects of violence need to find a way of negotiating various tensions. This sub-section suggests that data gathering should be looked to for more than the assessments derived. Instead it should be seen as a process of engagement. So in this regard, requiring the production of assessments about the burden of conflict is one way to ensure the bureaucratic machinery of the state is at least aware of problems often otherwise marginalized. In being made aware, officials can also receive a framework for making sense of what is going on and why. Information subsequently produced by officialdom – however questionable as a factual representation of the world – can be looked to a providing resources for a continuing 'facting'.

Questioning what is taken as known in order to examine the underlying assumptions being made is crucial to engagement. As suggested in Chapter 2, much of the disagreement about civilian deaths traded on notions about what constituted 'reliable' claims to knowledge. Standards of reliability were linked to alternative senses of the purpose of numbers: whether that was to set a precise figure, inform military operations, establish assistance requirements, acknowledge suffering, etc. Yet it is not just the British government that has brushed over the matter of what is being sought by 'reliability'.[24] Both those who have claimed that no authoritative figures were possible as well as those that have advanced their own estimates as authoritative have often sidelined the purposes for figures. Therefore, progressively questioning the presumptions behind estimates could provide one way of learning about the standards guiding commentators. It might also enable the transforming of what is deemed 'feasible'.

THE RULE OF LAW

As outlined in Chapter 3, one of the areas in which 'the facts' are supposed to matter is in the application of international humanitarian law (IHL). A foundational tenet of the law of armed conflict is that military necessity should be balanced against humanity. The need to find a compromise between these two principles in the conduct of operations is reflected in various rules (proportionality, indiscriminate attacks, superfluous injury). In stipulating the need for balance, in order to function as advertised the principles and rules of IHL require the collection and weighing of evidence about expected gains and costs of any attack.

One common response to the humanitarian harms is to seek greater relevance for international humanitarian law: enhanced adherence to the existing principles and rules, a refinement of their meaning, and a clarification of ambiguities. In relation to cluster munitions, for example, recent clarifications can be pointed to that provide a future path. In 2007, the former president of the self-declared Republic of Serbian Krajina (Milan Martić) was convicted of war crimes by the International Tribunal for the Former Yugoslavia.[25] Part of his sentence of 35 years imprisonment resulted from the use of a cluster munition rocket launcher (the M-87 Orkan) on Zagreb. The ruling has been welcomed by some legal commentators because the Tribunal concluded that, from the evidence presented to it, the distance of the attack and the characteristics of weapon rendered the M-87 Orkan 'indiscriminate'. This opens up the scope for future individual criminal responsibility in the use of certain cluster munitions in certain situations by establishing a precedent for determining what counts as indiscriminate.[26]

And yet, while IHL facilitates exchange about the rights and wrongs of conflict, this book has contended that it strictures it as well. The language provided by IHL has been a convenient one for governments to justify their actions and inactions.

The issue here is not simply the need for a rebalancing between military necessity and humanity. To speak in terms of recalculating or reweighing assumes that the proper authorities gather and consider evidence in a measured way – in other words, it assumes rigor in political accountability. As argued previously, the evidence supporting the 'balance' struck by certain nations on longstanding issues of controversy is weak to non-existent. While individual legal cases have been made against specific egregious uses of cluster munitions, this also stands in contrast to the past systematic lack of attention by countries such as the US, Russia, and the UK to their long term hazards. In some ways this situation is hardly surprising – the laws of war were established through an international system wherein nations have grossly unequal latitude to employ force.

So when a former US Air Force judge advocate cautioned against the further 'external influences' (read: international tribunals, NGOs) influencing where the balance gets stuck by writing the following, he perpetuated a belief required to maintain faith in balancing – that belligerent states routinely act in an informed manner:

> What is often forgotten is that the state-based process preserves the integrity of IHL's balance by facilitating discovery, whether through codification or practice, of where consensus lies. States are uniquely situated to perform the task since they are directly affected by decisions regarding military necessity and humanity.[27]

For the reasons given in this chapter and elsewhere then, caution must be exercised in looking to the rules and principles of IHL as a way of settling what is legitimate. By recounting efforts to negotiate the Convention on Cluster Munitions in Chapters 3 and 4, attention was given to the potential for international treaties to move beyond the bounds of the widely established IHL principles and rules. If those had been taken as the only basis for prohibiting cluster munitions, then nothing like the wide-ranging categorical ban agreed could have been justified. Yet, while the CCM was a political response to the limits of IHL, as a ratified international treaty it is now part of IHL. To be sure, it is not part of the canon of prescripts that non-signatories would accept as legally binding, but the CCM takes its place among the tapestry of international treaties. For those who choose to regard it as such, the CCM now stands as an accomplishment of IHL rather than a reflection of its disappointment.

This dynamic of incorporation indicates the way in which the failures of IHL can affirm its relevance. It also indicates the potential for dispute about what counts as IHL. As such, rather than looking to IHL as a set of rules that guards humanity in conflict, it can be understood as a site of contested possibilities. A question for consideration in line with the concerns of this book then, is: What does potential international law provide, not merely for refining, but instead for transforming, ideas about what counts as appropriate conduct?

In order to consider how this could be done, take the topic of cluster munitions again. Prior to their ban through the CCM, the dominant treatment of these weapons by governments was that they were similar to other weapons. It was argued that just as cluster munitions presented post-conflict dangers, so too would unitary bombs, shells, mortars, or other munitions that would be used in their place. As such, special controls could not be justified.

As Moyes has contended though, the ratification of the CCM provides the seeds to reverse this logic, to instead argue that the similarity of cluster munitions to other explosive weapons supports reappraising *explosive weapons* in general.[28] So in setting out what is banned, Article 2 of the CCM requires munitions to have five cumulative characteristics 'in order to avoid indiscriminate area effects and the risks posed by unexploded submunitions'. One of those includes the requirement that 'each explosive submunition is designed to detect and engage a single target object'; be that a vehicle, artillery piece, or another distinct item. Thus the CCM bans the use of submunitions that cause explosive force and fragmentation across an area without being able to limit effects *within* that overall area. In these ways, the distribution of explosive force across area is fundamental to the prohibition.

When read in combination with the prohibition in IHL against indiscriminate attack, the potential of Article 2 of the CCM could be quite sweeping. So Article 51 of the 1977 First Protocol Additional to the Geneva Conventions forbids attacks 'which employ a method or means of combat which cannot be directed at a specific military objective'. Again, Article 2 of the CCM defines indiscriminate as not being able to detect and engage a single target even within the overall area affected by submunitions. Therefore, the CCM questions the legality of any effects of explosive weapons that do not include measures to limit the effects to a single target. The potential promise of the category of explosive weapons will be examined further in the next chapter.

REVERSING THE ONUS

Given the far-ranging implications of interpreting the CCM as delegitimizing explosive weapons not limited to a single target, the prospects for this reading to become widely accepted by a sizable proportion of legal experts seems remote. What such thinking might well do though is to place a question mark over certain types of use of force by challenging conventional assumptions and arguments.

One way in which this could be facilitated is by reversing the onus of proof. As noted in Chapter 3, the starting point of much of IHL is that particular means of attack are permissible until proven otherwise. The weighing of military necessity and humanity specified in IHL represents a cost–benefit assessment. Military commanders are entrusted with determining the appropriateness of force on a case-by-case basis in light of the particulars of each situation. As such, justifying a categorical prohibition would require a convincing demonstration that specific weapons violate a rule of IHL across the range of anticipated scenarios. By prohibiting the employment of laser weapons specifically designed to blind out of concerns that such devices would cause superfluous injury to troops, the 1995 Protocol IV to the Convention on Certain Conventional Weapons stands as one example of such a categorical prohibition. Yet, such instances are rare.

The CCM broke with this traditional manner for handling the burden of proof. Herein, the starting orientation was that those states wishing to make exclusions from prohibition were the ones that had to justify why. As argued in Chapter 3, as a strategy this shifting was inspired by the need for and facilitated an escape from the weighing logic of IHL.

Contrast the CCM to other recent initiatives. Since at least 2003, campaigners, states, and inter-governmental organizations have been debating the merits of creating an international treaty framework for controlling the trade of conventional weapons. Since 2006, the idea of an 'Arms Trade Treaty' has been promoted within the United Nations. In 2012, a major conference will be held to agree a legally binding instrument. In advance of that event, at the time of writing, a series of Preparatory Committee meetings are taking place. In July 2011, the Chair's draft paper for the text of the treaty included a variety of criteria for the authorization of exports. For instance, states would not be able to approve a transfer, among other things, 'if there is a substantial risk that those conventional arms would:

1. Be used in a manner that would seriously undermine peace and security or, provoke, prolong or aggravate internal, regional, subregional or international instability.
2. Be used to commit or facilitate serious violations of international humanitarian law.

3. Be used to commit or facilitate serious violations of international human rights law.'[29]

The onus of proof will be critical to the meaning and relevance of these and other criteria. At the time of writing, the Arms Trade Treaty does not provide guidance about how assessment of risk should be conducted, merely that states should undertake them against the criteria specified. But it matters enormously in relation to transfers of concern, for example, whether a positive case has to be made by governments that a certain export is likely to be used inappropriately in the future or whether past experience demonstrated by others can justify an initial presumption of risk unless reasons can be given otherwise.

The burden of proof is not just a factor within formal international treaties. Instead it is a pervasive feature of debates about what is right or wrong, legitimate and illegitimate, permissible and impermissible. So in the disputes about Iraqi civilians killed, the UK government did not regard itself as having to make a case for how many people died, or even a case for why it was not possible to make estimates. Instead, it responded to others' figures by (on certain occasions) pointing to the disparity between calculations based on different methodologies gauging different types of deaths (though not acknowledging this) in order to contend that 'reliable' estimates could not be produced.

Finding ways of reversing the onus of proof can be a powerful move in reducing the harms of state violence and the opacity of statecraft. Within environmental movements, this has been one of the elements often associated with 'precautionary approaches' to risk.[30] But reversing the onus is in itself only an initial orientation to arguments. It does not settle what counts as credible evidence, what needs to be proven in the first place, or what to do in the absence of necessary information. Perhaps more profoundly is the matter of the harm needed to justify a rethink. The CCM may have operated with the starting assumption that the retention of any cluster munitions needed to be argued for, but this was only done after decades of death and injury.

Other possible dangers can be identified. Many of the 'pre-emptive' national security policies adopted in the US after 9/11 were justified through much of the same logic used by those advocating precautionary approaches to environmental policies.[31] Among other things, the Bush Administration contended that Iraq had to prove it no longer posed a WMD threat in order to avoid intervention.

Still another danger is that the heightened scrutiny given by reversing the onus for one set of issues may cast disproportionate attention on a narrow set of humanitarian concerns. For instance, to start with a presumption that certain weapons are 'indiscriminate' until proven otherwise could result in other options being used that are just as worrisome. To acknowledge this is not to endorse the hypothetical and empty hand-waving of officials detailed in Chapter 3. Rather, it is to recognize the need for careful consideration that attempts to 'humanize' certain aspects of conflict might unintentionally legitimate other forms of violence.[32] They may also undermine efforts to work towards the elimination of war.[33]

Shifting burdens, then, is not so much a decision rule for resolving what should be done, but rather an orientation in approaching troublesome topics. It can provide argumentative resources for compelling states to better justify their actions and inactions. But how that should happen and when are inseparable from judgments formed by our reflections and interventions. So, in relation to civilian deaths, previous chapters have justified doubt regarding the substance backing up occasional pronouncements given by some nations. Therefore, activities that lead to a shifting in the onus for proof as part of current international efforts might well be productive. A driving purpose of such elaborations would not necessarily be to resolve the facts, but rather to set in train practical steps and possibilities for questioning. How figures should be calculated, by whom, and for what audience are still questions that need to be addressed in light of working assessments about what would be useful in order to avoid suffering in the future.

STIGMA BUILDING

Just as shifting the onus of proof is intertwined with what gets taken for granted and what gets questioned, so too is the building of norms, stigma, and taboos on violence. In recent years within the field of International Relations, a great deal of interest has been directed at understanding how conceptions of what is acceptable bear on what actions are undertaken. Norms can be thought of as shared standards of right and wrong that influence behavior and identity.[34] They do so by generating expectations about the consequences or appropriateness of acts. For instance, the acquisition of high-tech weaponry by some nations has been explained as stemming from their perceptions of what it means to be a modern state rather than from strategic defense calculations.[35,36]

One of the starkest areas for norms, stigma, and taboos in international affairs is in relation to the themes of this book: the conduct of state violence. When the possession and use of certain weapons is seen as incompatible with the identity a country wishes to foster in the international community, then this has contributed to restraint. Some of the most destructive weapons have been rendered effectively out of bounds because of international standards about what constitutes acceptable action.

Take the case of the Anti-Personnel Mine (APM) Ban Convention. The 1997 APM Ban Convention forbids the use, production, acquisition, and transfer of anti-personnel mines. Over 150 countries have signed up to this prohibition, but this does not include major military powers such as the US, Russia, China, India, and Pakistan. This lack of universal inclusion might be taken as a major deficiency. However this conclusion would ignore the contribution of the Convention in setting informal international standards.[37] This is so because:

> [M]ost of the 41 states that are not party to the Treaty are in practice respecting its prohibitions on their transfer, production and use. This can be attributed to the stigmatization of these weapons in the eyes of the public. In the increasingly rare cases where some of these states have used antipersonnel mines, reaction has been swift and vigorous.[38]

The US, for instance, 'has not used antipersonnel mines since 1991, exported them since 1992, or produced them since 1997'.[39] The worldwide export and shipment of APMs has also been reduced dramatically with the APM Ban Convention. Thirteen states not signed up to it have still initiated a moratorium on the trade of these mines. This example illustrates how international agreements can have relevance beyond those officially signed up to them.

The modern history of attempts to proscribe chemical weapons indicates how international deliberations, declarations, and treaties can have implications beyond their binding requirements. Both before and after the first use of chlorine gas in warfare by the Germans at Ypres in World War I, the militaries and publics of western Europe voiced concern about the appropriateness of such weapons. Among the many new means of mass killing developed during World War I, chemical weapons were set apart from others.[40] After the war this differentiation continued. Both opponents and proponents of chemical warfare contended it was distinctive and particularly powerful.[41] Opponents portrayed this weaponry as inhumane in large part because of its supposedly indiscriminate effects. Proponents portrayed it as leading to fewer casualties, as their destructive capability would ensure a swift conclusion to conflict.[42]

As Richard Price has argued, the repeated reinforcement of the stigma against chemical weapons through international negotiations and public anxiety played an important role in shaping perceptions about their utility and acceptability within militaries up to World War II.[43] It was not simply the case that past prohibitions (such as the Hague Conference of 1899) were irrelevant because they were violated, or weak because they were subject to qualification. Rather, over time the repeated portrayal of chemical weapons as 'beyond the pale' had wide-ranging consequences for how their ultimate utility was conceived.[44] Their perceived lack of fit with 'military culture' prior to World War II meant that nations were reluctant to dedicate resources to these options which, in turn, meant they did not achieve the military effectiveness they might have done.

After World War II, the view that chemical weapons were unacceptable for a modern state became increasingly widespread.[45] Today, that some countries might use, proliferate, possess, or even be suspected of possessing such weapons can (at least on some occasions) lead to a significant response. For example, that the Iraqi military employed chemical weapons to kill over 5,000 Iraqi Kurds in Halabja and elsewhere during 1988 was widely cited in the lead up to the 2003 Iraq war (though not nearly as much in 1988 when many Western nations favored Iraq in the conflict with Iran) as an indication of Saddam Hussein's rogue status. Through such arguments, chemical weapons have been placed in an especially repugnant moral category.[46]

Different theories have been offered regarding how norms become consequential or important.[47] Within scholarly debates, the question has been posed of whether a particular norm is followed because it resonates with other norms, because of its place within the hierarchy of norms,[48] or because of its specificity.[49] Some have strongly opposed the suggestion that the uptake of a norm should be understood in terms of their resonance with other ones[50] or that norms produce identity in any clear-cut manner. The emphasis instead is on how some individuals persuade others about what matters.[51]

Through rendering some uses of force as problematic, generating norms is one strategy for attempting to reduce the humanitarian casualties and consequences of state violence. In the future, the

CCM might have implications beyond those states that have adopted it and far beyond its formal terms.[52] Perhaps in recognition of this, in late 2011, the US repeatedly sought in vain to advance a new international protocol under the CCW. Through achieving international sign-up to an agreement highly permissive regarding the retention of cluster munitions, this CCW protocol could well have undermined and muddled the standards established under the CCM. In 2011 NGOs, inter-governmental organizations, and others successfully marshaled their expertise and capabilities to work against the US-led international agreement (one that might well have included major military powers such as Russia, India, and China) in large part because of its effects on the perceived *de facto* standards established by the CCM.

Due to the manner in which it closes off what is acceptable, stigmatization stands as something of the opposite to the previous strategy of demanding elaborations of proof. Just as there are dangers associated with shifting the onus, so too are there with stigmatization. As with conventions about what is right or wrong, norms can reinforce otherwise questionable beliefs about what is acceptable. For instance, what have traditionally been labeled as 'unconventional' weapons – nuclear, biological, and chemical weapons – have been subject to much attention in recent times. That they kill and injure in ways unlike traditional kinetic-force weapons is one of the reasons why they have been deemed insidious and inhumane. Yet, with this growing international apprehension, a danger is that conventional weapons become more and more normalized as 'conventional' – even if they can kill and maim to degrees comparable to nuclear, biological or chemical means. For instance, fuel-air explosives might have the destructive power of small nuclear weapons, but they have not been subject to anything like the same level of moral scrutiny.[53]

Conversely, some have argued that norms can impede the development of more 'humane' force options. Under an exemption provided in the Chemical Weapons Convention for 'law enforcement including domestic riot control' situations, some armed forces (for instance, in the US and Russia) are actively pursuing novel 'incapacitating' chemical agents for military operations other than war. The often-stated justification is to find ways of handling situations short of the resort to lethal force. However, others maintain that the development of new options could well undermine attempts to categorically eliminate chemical weapons *per se*.[54] Whatever the merits of each side, stigma makes it problematic for both proponents and detractors to openly debate such possibilities. For proponents of these agents this is so because even if such weapons were deemed appropriate within international treaty law, they could be seen as advocating the use of tainted chemical weapons. For detractors this is so because engaging in debate about rights and wrong could unravel the instinctive condemnation of options that resemble chemical weapons.

In addition, some commentators have maintained that the attention to unconventional weapons has not only been selective, but also self-serving. That biological and chemical weapons have been subject to treaties and international standards, making their possession illegitimate but the stockpiling of nuclear weapons is still legitimate (for some states), has been taken as emblematic of the uneven distribution of geopolitical power.[55]

Moving beyond 'unconventional' weapons, the emerging norms associated with APMs and cluster munitions indicate a fairly recent turn to stigmatizing conventional weapons. The next chapter speaks to the selectivity of stigmatization by asking how standards of right or wrong could develop in relation to explosive weapons in populated areas. In doing so, it builds on a sense of mindfulness cultivated in this chapter regarding the dilemmas and possibilities of redressing the machinations of statecraft.

6
Framing and Framed:
The Category of Explosive Violence

In developing a concept of a negotiated relation between disclosure, concealment, knowledge, and ignorance, Part II asked what possibilities exist for understanding and intervening in the practice of statecraft. This chapter considers that co-development of agendas in relation to a specific topic, by approaching violence through the notion of 'frame'.

This concept refers to the set of organizing principles that encourages assessments (and discourage others) of what is going on, why, what needs doing, and by whom. In other words, frames are the analytical lenses through which we interpret the world. As such, the framing of issues is as pervasive as it is disputable. In turning attention in certain directions and not others, ways of seeing provide selective and partial simplifications. These characteristics make frames both enabling and constraining as well as necessary and questionable.

Framing is undertaken here in relation to the use of 'explosive violence' and 'explosive weapons'. One of the goals is to ask about the choices and challenges facing emerging efforts to mobilize attention to the harms caused by armed violence. In doing so, this chapter offers a next turn in the conversation about what can be done. A second goal is to move on from that initial frame at the level of the use of force by considering how the category of 'explosive weapons' itself can be framed.

FRAMING THE BASICS

As with many widespread concepts in the social sciences, the meaning given to 'frame' varies. At its center is the idea that people are not blank slates, but rather that we have preconceived notions about how to make sense of events.[1] Walter Lippmann referred to frames as 'the pictures in our heads' by which we interpret the world. Reese and colleagues called them the 'organizing principles that are socially shared and persistent over time'.[2] Gamson and

Modigliani defined frames as the central ideas for structuring our sense of events and what is at issue.[3]

Frames are not just in our head, but written in our words. The portrayal of events in the media or by politicians is often directed through a recognizable frame. When an unarmed demonstrator is killed during the policing of a demonstration, for instance, much depends on how the issue is depicted. It might be presented as a single event where confusion or chance loomed large. Or it could be linked to a sense of history – for example, the inadequacies of monitoring procedures or a failure to sanction officers for past wrongdoing. It is through the contest of frames that those 'who are most effective in establishing causal background may be able to control public assessment of blame'.[4]

Thus, by providing a way of understanding, frames define problems, identify causes, and suggest recommendations. Take the issue of crime. Through slogans, imagery, and headlines, the rate of crime can be seen as the result of:

- *Blocked Opportunities*: Social inequalities and discrimination that calls for attention to root causes in society;
- *Social Breakdown*: Family or community collapse that requires a revitalization of these institutions;
- *Faulty Justice System*: A criminal justice system that has become too lenient; or
- *Media Violence*: Widespread aggressive images that need to be curtailed.[5]

Such ways of structuring enable an understanding of a complex topic while also simplifying it by bringing some issues to the fore. For the first crime-frame, an individual's background and their social and economic opportunities are prominent, whereas they are not relevant for the third. Through organizing understanding, some people are deemed as victims, others as perpetrators, and others as culpable. In the way in which frames hide while making visible, they epitomize many of the dynamics discussed elsewhere in this book regarding the interrelation of concealment and disclosure.

The pervasiveness (and elusiveness) of framing is suggested by noting the many dimensions along which they figure. Events, topics, and people can all be framed. For each, this could happen at different levels.[6] So the attacks of September 11, 2001 can be framed in terms of their meaning and also how they enter into other wider understandings. To treat that day as entailing a declaration of war rather than a succession of criminal acts suggests what response was most important: counterforce. In this way, September 11, 2001 became part of the George W. Bush administration's 'war on terror'.

The 'war on terror' represents a stark example of a frame. By repeatedly characterizing counter-terrorism activities under this title, the Bush Administration promoted military-centered responses. Moreover, other countries were asked to choose between 'us' and 'them'. The term 'terrorism' under this call acted to aggregate together violent acts that in the past may well have been regarded as distinct. The imperative of being engaged in war was used to justify huge financial expenditure – as similar to the US 'war on drugs' and the 'war on cancer'. Wars in general and the 'war on terrorism' in particular are often said to require national unity and patriotic fervor. Unity was also promoted on the international stage, as nations with a previously strained relation to the US (such as Russia and Pakistan) became symbolically linked partners in a united cause.

While frames can provide an organizing rationale for the national mobilization of ideas and materials, they also matter in more subtle respects. So by offering diagnoses of problems and related solutions, frames are part and parcel of attempts to propose what points about a topic are salient and what ways of thinking are helpful.[7] In representing the beginning of the war in Afghanistan in 2001, for instance, the news broadcasters Al Jazeera and CNN operated with different organizing principles. The former frequently employed humanitarian frames that identified the toll of the conflict on individuals while avoiding subscribing to the language of terrorism. In contrast, CNN concentrated on the effectiveness of military operations and technology while using 'terrorism' unproblematically.[8]

The manner in which frames provide the basis for contrasting interpretations of events makes them the very stuff of politics. Without some sort of organizing simplifications, it would be impossible to make sense of the world. But attending to only some parts can serve to reinforce dubious or preconceived thinking. So a concern for this book is how to engage the partial disclosing that is framing, while also asking how frames confine possibilities.

FRAMING THE USE OF FORCE

How then can we choose to make sense of violence and, in particular, state violence? What aspects of it are worth focusing on? If the minimization of harms from conflict to civilian populations is taken as a shared goal, then which of the many possibilities for doing this should be promoted?

As indicated by previous chapters, one of the standard ways of trying to remedy the harms of conflict has been to control its means – in other words, regulating or banning the weapons of war.[9] To name but a few, formal restrictions of varying kinds have been placed on incendiary, chemical, and biological weapons as well as mines. In addition, international civil society has sought to introduce regulatory and legal controls on the access to small arms. Today, in the media and elsewhere, much of the political attention is directed towards novel weapons such as dense inert metal explosives (DIME), depleted uranium, and white phosphorous. It is certainly possible to imagine further international initiatives to proscribe them in the future.

As expressed by those emphasizing 'explosive violence', a stated goal is to achieve a 'reframing of conventional attitudes to weapons and violence'.[10] Explosive weapons include artillery shells, missiles, bombs (mortar bombs, aircraft bombs, suicide bombs), grenades, landmines, and rockets. What unites this diverse range of technologies is that they function by projecting an area-blast from an explosion in order to inflict injury, damage, and death.

An initial move made as part of the recent attention to this category has been to maintain that harms to civilians and damage to infrastructure from explosive weapons – especially when they are used in populated areas – are readily foreseeable. In short, there is a pattern. Air strikes in Georgia, grenades in Nigeria, artillery attacks in Gaza, shelling in Yemen, and improvized explosive devices in Baghdad produce patterns of significant harm.

An initial attempt at sketching that pattern was given in 2006 by the NGOs Landmine Action and Medact when they compiled a database of incidents involving the use of such weapons based on English-language media reports over a six-month period.[11] They concluded, for instance, that:

- Of a total of 1,836 incidents in some 58 countries or territories, the total minimum reported killed was 6,115 and the minimum reported wounded was 12,670.
- Civilians were involved in 64 percent of incidents (1,180), comprising 69 percent of the total reported killed (4,237) and 83 percent of the total reported wounded (10,556).

- Incidents in populated areas[12] presented significantly higher average numbers of killed and wounded per incident than those in non-populated areas. The average number reported killed in attacks in populated areas was almost twice as high as in unpopulated ones, while the average number reported wounded was more than three times higher.
- 83 percent of those killed and 90 percent of those injured in attacks in populated areas were civilians.

While recognizing limitations with the data, the argument was forwarded that the human costs of such incidents were substantial. For survivors, immediate injuries include amputations, blindness, loss of hearing, and brain trauma. After recovery from the initial injuries, discrimination and economic exclusion can follow. Less visible than direct deaths, the welfare of populations becomes compromised when vital infrastructure – such as medical, power, water, and sanitation facilities – gets targeted. Since that initial work in 2006, other studies have offered similar patterns of harm.[13]

Such conclusions about the pattern of effects were echoed in a 2009 report to the UN Security Council. In it the UN Secretary-General wrote of the severe humanitarian concerns associated with explosive weapons with area effects in densely populated areas (as witnessed in Sri Lanka and Gaza).[14] In July 2010, the UN Under-Secretary-General for Humanitarian Affairs and Emergency Relief Coordinator likewise stated that:

> The use of 'ordinary' explosive weapons in populated areas also repeatedly causes unacceptably high levels of harm to civilians. From air strikes and artillery attacks in Afghanistan, Somalia, Yemen and Gaza to rockets launched at Israeli civilian areas by Palestinian militants and car bombs and suicide attacks in Pakistan or Iraq, use of explosive weapons and explosives has resulted in severe civilian suffering.[15]

March 2011 saw high-level UN reiteration of concerns about explosive weapons in statements by the Coordinator of UN Emergency Relief regarding the shelling and bombardment of populated civilian areas in Libya[16] and Ivory Coast.[17] The former conflict would inextricably be defined by this category of weapons. The explicit justification for NATO intervention was the protection of civilians and much of this stemmed from concerns about explosive weapons being used against population centers such as Benghazi and

Misrata. A major plank of NATO's military response included the bombing of targets in or near populated areas. Ghaddafi forces laid anti-personnel and anti-vehicle landmines, fired cluster munitions, and launched rockets in or near residential areas.[18] In July 2011, the International Committee of the Red Cross drew attention to concerns regarding the effects of these weapons on health-care facilities operating in conflict situations.[19]

In attaching a general pattern to an overarching category of weaponry, such critical scrutiny seeks to 'reframe' existing discussions at multiple levels. In terms of topics, it directs attention to what is normally deemed as 'conventional'. The focus is not with relatively exotic weapons such as white phosphorous, but rather with de-naturalizing those standard force options in arsenals around the world.

In terms of the nature of the problem at stake, the identification of a pattern of harm shifts attention away from individual attacks. Deaths and damage from explosive weapons in populated areas cannot be dismissed as simply due to 'human error', 'technical faults', 'the fog of war', or some other extenuating factor as so often portrayed in media accounts.[20] Instead they should be expected. The shift away from attending to specific instances (what is called an 'episodic framing') to general conditions (what is called a 'thematic framing') indicates the breadth of what is needed to redress harms. This is not simply a matter that should be left to commanders in the field; responsibility lies elsewhere too.[21]

However, in the current attention to explosive weapons, the reframing of violence is not just based on findings regarding effects from previous conflicts. It is also based on a sense of widely shared standards. Explosive weapons are already treated in practice as a coherent, taken-for-granted category despite the diversity of the technologies covered by the term. So they rarely figure within the context of domestic law enforcement. When this happens – as is the case of the Mexican government's response to drug cartels – it is typically regarded as a breakdown of law and order. Instead, explosive weapons are overwhelmingly used by military forces in the context of external or internal armed conflict. The latter, too, is typically regarded as a failure of state authority. This treatment differs from firearms which also cause death and injury but that are widely accepted as force options for the military and the police.

Once this categorical management across different settings is recognized, it is possible to ask whether it is appropriate. Who should be put at risk of injury would seem to turn on political accountability. States do not use these weapons when they are directly accountable to the populations that might be adversely affected by them. With a view to reducing humanitarian harm, the question could be asked: If explosive weapons are generally regarded as intolerable to use within a national border, when – and why – should they be tolerable elsewhere? Especially in situations that fall short of outright battlefield warfare (which would include most of what is termed as 'armed conflict' today), why should it be permissible for only some people to be put at risk?[22]

The thrust of this questioning shares similarities with certain strands of contemporary military thinking. Through the prism of the tactical effectiveness of counterinsurgency operations, the need has been expressed to rethink the accountability of military forces to local populations. General Stanley McChrystal's directives in mid-2009 to the International Security Assistance Force in Afghanistan to avoid civilian deaths is one such example. As a matter of policy, what was sought was a rejection of any tidy separation between 'military effectiveness' and 'humanity'. Achieving the former required attending to the latter. As part of the change of policy, NATO was presented as accepting greater responsibility for deaths.[23] Effective counterinsurgency was not held as achievable simply by more force, better technology, or speedier responses. Instead, the accountability of militaries to the populations they are meant to protect was presented as paramount.

Current efforts to recognize 'explosive weapons' as a coherent category then stand in complex relation to dominant assumptions in the practices of states. Through providing a particular way of seeing long-standing concerns, some forms of normalcy are denied while others are built upon.

TECHNOLOGY AND RECOGNITION

By directing attention about the use of force at a category of technology, recent efforts with respect to explosive weapons have sought to foster a particular definition of the problem: attention is on *what* is used rather than *who* acts or necessarily *how*. The focus on a group of technologies as the source of the problem is both consequential and contingent.

The consequential aspects of it can be seen in the way categories are fought over. For instance, as part of its formal rejection of the 1997 Mine Ban Treaty, the US government has argued that not all anti-personnel mines are the same. It has attempted to carve a space for so-called 'smart' self-destructing (sometimes 'non-lethal') mines. The aim is to distinguish the general category of 'anti-personnel landmines' into subcategories such as 'smart' versus 'persistent' ones so as to open a space for new mine options. The promotion of the category of explosive weapons seeks the opposite result: to group a wide range of technologies together for the purpose of narrowing down the space for otherwise 'legal' force to cause harm.

One advantage of the explosive weapons agenda is that by placing technology front and center, many of the political sensitivities that delimit criticism on the international stage can be circumvented. Attention is directed away from claim and counter-claim about the intent of allies or adversary states, and instead towards a technical capability that many states and non-state actors share. In addition, this focus could build on the preoccupation (often bordering on fascination) with military technology that is so common in Western journalism and officialdom.

With such advantages come points for caution too. In terms of intent, while focusing on technology can circumvent the frequent reluctance of states to overtly criticize each other, intent is sometimes regarded as paramount in the use of force. States such as the US, Russia, and Israel frequently distinguish deaths from their force from that of others through reference to intent. As a result, an exclusive focus on technology is, at least at times, liable to generate a hostile response. Likewise, trying to harness the mass media's preoccupation with technology could ultimately result in political questions about the legitimacy of force being diluted. By casting discussion about technology, it would hardly be surprising if governments responded – as in the past for anti-personnel mines or cluster munitions – with proposals for 'better weapons': those that are more accurate, reliable, etc. A critical question is whether such proposals amount to inadequate technical patches to problems that ultimately stem from systematic failures of political accountability.[24]

The contingent aspects of this category relate to its coherence. Especially given the diversity of weapons that fit under the heading of 'explosive weapons' – even if it is accepted that there is a general pattern of effects – to group them all together invites questions as to whether this can be justified. Exactly how what is used, by who, in which circumstances, against whom, with what sorts of precautions, and so on, could all be cited as reasons for casting doubt on any attempt to accept this grouping as coherent.

While the breadth of weapons covered by the wide net cast by the term 'explosive weapons' may present challenges if the goal is to definitively represent inherent capabilities, it can be an advantage in fostering dialogue. So, once the category is accepted as a legitimate one of humanitarian concern, related disputes about what should rightly be included could be highly productive. For instance, in relation to themes in the previous two chapters regarding the onus of proof, states could be challenged to reveal their evidence regarding why some weapons should be excluded from this classification. The quality and quantity of evidence to support such distinctions is likely to be telling – and not just in relation to this single grouping of weapons.

Challenges as to what should be included within the category itself helps cement its relevance. Consider in this respect the history of so-called 'non-lethal weapons'. The search for differential force options has a long history. In the past decades, weapons such as tear gas, water cannons, and rubber bullets were advanced as appropriate for dealing with public disorder. Later options of this ilk included chemical sprays and electroshock devices. By the mid-1990s though, a variety of military and police commentators advanced the label of 'non-lethal weapons' as a unifying term.[25] Under it fell the previously mentioned weapons as well as 'next generation' ones, such as directed energy, calmative agents, and acoustic devices.[26] Together these diverse weapons were taken as manifestations of the desire to find options short of lethal force. Funding applications, publications, an international conference circuit, and even some innovations followed.

Much of the skeptical attention has been directed at debunking the notion that these weapons were, in fact, really 'non-lethal'.[27] The placement of quotations around the term, for instance, has been used to question its accuracy. Counter responses to this skeptical position have contended that while death might sometimes result, the goal was to avoid this outcome by providing options short of firearms. Variant designations such as 'less-lethal' and 'less-than-lethal' were offered to acknowledge the possibility for fatalities while signaling the underlining intent.

As a participant in these discussions, over time it became my assessment that in shoehorning itself around 'lethal' labels, skeptical attention was being directed at one end of the force spectrum. Evidence suggested that many such weapons were being deployed in situations far beyond those where the use of firearms would be considered acceptable.[28] Counter-labels such as 'more-than-before weapons' or 'pain weapons' though – the experiences in Cairo's Tahrir Square in the autumn of 2011 offered a recent illustration of the relevance of such designations – did not gain widespread traction. Efforts to simply reject the 'non-lethal' label were arguably too few.[29] Instead, through the acceptance of 'lethal' as the focal point for debate, in funding applications, publications, and an international conference circuit, many proponents and critics together perpetuated a slanted debate.

As such, it is necessary to be mindful of the implications of using categories. Those drawing attention to 'explosive weapons' at present – as with other attempts to define problems – are listening for echoes. By promoting a framing of the use of force through the promotion of a new category, the hope is that others will take it up and start using it in communications. At the time of writing, that is a conversation that was initiated by NGOs with some inter-governmental agencies and a limited number of officials. The category will need to be adopted much more widely if it is to have a practical bearing on armed violence. Within this expansion of voices, criticism can function as a form of buy-in. So, nuclear weapons might be offered as the most extreme case of an explosive weapon. Whether its 'unconventional' features make it dissimilar enough to fall outside the proper scope of 'explosive weapons' is a debatable point. But a debate about this point would still work to reinforce the salience of a category that is not widely recognized today.

However, much of the international attention on explosive weapons to date has not been solely directed at technology. During a November 22, 2010 UN Security Council open debate on the protection of civilians, the European Union, Mexico, Australia, and others pitched their concern in terms of the use of these weapons in concentrations of civilian populations. In June 2011, under the umbrella International Network on Explosive Weapons, the NGOs Action on Armed Violence, Handicap International, Human Rights Watch, IKV Pax Christi, Medact, Norwegian People's Aid, Oxfam, and Save the Children called on states and other actors to:

- Acknowledge that the use of explosive weapons in populated areas tends to cause severe harm to individuals and communities and furthers suffering by damaging vital infrastructure;
- Strive to avoid such harm and suffering in any situation, review and strengthen national policies and practices on the use of explosive weapons, and gather and make available relevant data;

- Work for full realization of the rights of victims and survivors; and
- Develop stronger international standards, including certain prohibitions and restrictions on the use of explosive weapons in populated areas.

Such formulations are likely to invite discussion directed around the question of how much of the problem is related to 'the technology' versus 'the context' of their use. Ambiguity about this could be a constructive way to generate debate and analysis while promoting recognition of the category of explosive weapons.[30]

FRAMING EXPLOSIVE WEAPONS

Attempting to secure recognition for the category of explosive weapons, creates the potential for making problematic what was unevenly regarded as so in the past. In identifying a problem, specifying why it is a problem, and diagnosing the reasons for it, these emerging efforts provide a frame for making sense of violence. And yet, at least at the time of writing, many of those organizations directing attention to explosive weapons have stopped short of offering a set of specific solutions for what needs doing – such as the revision of rules of engagement, political declarations of non-use, new international laws, transparency requirements, etc. Instead, attention has been focused on building awareness and debate. Proving a prognosis though, is often one of the central functions of frames and, in any case, vital in achieving reform.[31]

Partly in order to consider what needs doing, the remainder of this chapter shifts on from efforts to identify an issue of concern to instead ask how that concern should be characterized. Possible options are outlined with a view to asking what they enable as well as foreclose. The hope is that doing so will sharpen awareness of what is at stake in the selective portrayal of the framing issue.

Consider, in this regard, one set of possibilities for characterizing explosive weapons: international humanitarian law frames. In placing limits on the means and methods of warfare through stipulating that military necessity must be balanced by humanity, in its own fashion IHL provides a way of organizing controversy about armed conflict, be it in relation to explosive weapons, mines, incendiary devices, depleted uranium, etc.

In general terms, the rules and principles of IHL direct attention to individual attacks: the precautions taken and the consequences that result. As the ICRC forwarded in late 2011:

> The permissibility of reliance on [explosive weapons] must therefore be determined on a case-by-case basis, taking into account IHL rules prohibiting indiscriminate and disproportionate attacks, and imposing obligations to take feasible precautions in attack.[32]

In this sort of IHL-indebted framing, the distinction between non-combatants and combatants is of considerable importance. In the case of the former, incidental loss of life and objects is to not be excessive in relation to the military advantage of attacks. In the case of combatants, unnecessary suffering must be avoided. To the question of what needs doing, using IHL as a lens places much importance on compelling compliance with rules and refining their meaning. In doing so, law as a field of study is the core body of knowledge that is required. Some states and NGOs have sought to question the acceptability of explosive weapons through reference to the rules of IHL, particularly those related to the prohibition of 'indiscriminate' attacks.[33]

As suggested in previous chapters, while it might act to identify and deter egregious acts, structuring understanding through the rules and principles of IHL has proven limiting. In part this has stemmed from uncertainty and disagreement about what should be counted (and how) within attempts to find a 'balance'. More fundamentally, in practice, the demands of rules in place have proven hallow in relation to achieving an informed balancing. The evidence-base supporting determinations of where the point of balance lies are often obscure, thin, or simply non-existent. In addition, the importance given to the law can act as a barrier to non-legalistic arguments about what needs doing. Such deficiencies suggest that it would be unwise to use the language and parameters of IHL to characterize what is at stake with explosive weapons.

Of course, it would be possible to modify IHL. As is prevalent in legal studies today, it could be combined with other aspects of law in order to promote different ways of making sense of conflict. International human rights law, for instance, is being looked to by some as offering more rigorous and more widely applicable standards for conflict.[34] Through such efforts, explosive weapons could be reevaluated. Alternatively, it could be argued that while the use of explosive weapons in populated areas might not always fall foul of the letter of IHL, such acts do violate its spirit.[35]

EXPLOSIVE WEAPONS AS A PUBLIC HEALTH PROBLEM

In what follows, I want to move on from legal-inspired ways of understanding to consider another set of possibilities: public-health framings. There is no definite sense of what constitutes a public-health framing. As an initial orientation though, this calls for not treating individual instances in isolation. Instead, patterns of events must be established in order to derive measures to prevent or lessen identified concerns. More specifically, the organizing principles that might be associated with such framings[36] include:

- Addressing problems at the level of populations and the implications for their quality of life, rather than limiting attention to individuals and deaths;
- The need to combine different fields (including epidemiology, education, ethics, sociology, economics, and psychology);
- A focus on the prevention of harms to all and on the protection of identified vulnerable groups;
- A systematic evidence-based approach that calls for the collection of data to establish the size, scope, characteristics, and consequences of harms;
- An identification of the risk factors and root causes of harm; and
- The undertaking of a range of interventions and an evaluation of their effectiveness.

Such principles differ from those associated with IHL. The latter amounted to a legalistic assessment of the balance of damages and benefits from specific attacks that (in practice) has been done with something far less than systematic evidencing.

Especially over the last decade, public-health framings have been advanced for a number of topics. In relation to day-to-day social violence, many have sought to move beyond criminal justice-based approaches that focus on policing and punishment.[37] For the World Health Organization a public health approach seeks to answer:

the questions, 'who are the victims and perpetrators of violence?'; 'what are the causes of the different types of violence?'; 'how do the different types of violence vary from context to context?' and 'how can we use this knowledge to reduce the frequency with which people use violence against one another?'. It addresses the underlying societal, community and relationship factors that exert a long-term influence on the likelihood of individuals behaving violently toward other individuals. It also addresses the situational factors that exert a short-term influence on the likelihood of violence taking place (and on the amount of physical and psychosocial harm inflicted), and the post-incident factors that influence the severity and extent of the physical, mental and social harm following violence.[38]

Along these lines, much effort in recent years has sought to identify risk factors and entry points for the prevention of armed conflict,[39] with special emphasis on small arms.[40] In the case of gambling, a public-health framing has been developed to move beyond conceiving of addiction as a form of individual pathology and of enjoyment as a matter of individual freedom.[41]

Public-health framings support certain messages for communication over others:

- Those that include reference to prevention and root causes over those looking at the legality of individual incidents;
- Those that bring attention to long-term and indirect consequences rather that just short-term and direct ones;
- Those that draw a connection between past and current usages over those limited to the latter;
- Those that attend to the political accountability of users to local populations over those that present attacks in operational terms; and
- Those that ask why less contentious practices typically associated with traditional policing are not employed.

The general orientation given above shares many affinities with the previous discussion about explosive weapons. The call to question the who, what, how, and when of problems is in line with building debate and an understanding of what kind of issues are at stake. The importance within public-health framings of acknowledging a broad range of social and economic consequences is in line with the desire to build an expansive understanding of the direct and indirect damages from these weapons to individuals, families, communities, and societies.

CHOICES AND PURPOSES

With the value attached to gathering systematic evidence and evaluating options, public-health framings can provide the bases for bringing greater attention to explosive weapons while providing the grounds for revising the understanding of what problems are associated with them.[42] The lenses of public-health support concerted attention to questions such as: 'What is the range of short- and long-term consequences associated with explosive weapons?', 'Are some groups more at risk than others?', and 'How can greater knowledge about explosive weapons be used to reduce the intensity and frequency of their use?'.[43]

More than just noting such general affinities, the remainder of this chapter examines the purposes aided by this choice of framing.

Because public-health casts concern at the level of populations, one of the things that distinguishes such framings from typical humanitarian ones is impartiality with regard to who suffers. Explosive weapons can have debilitating effects on military personnel and combatants that last far beyond a conflict. Acknowledging this as part of the framing of explosive weapons could support the creation of a wide coalition of concern. So, much of the emerging focus on 'explosive weapons' at the international level today, is directed toward the protection of civilians. Yet, particularly over the last decade, technologies that fall under this label have gained a high prominence for many Western governments, veterans associations, and health-service agencies. Improvised explosive devices, for instance, have caused considerable injury and death to combatants. Recognizing this extended range of suffering could be used to promote collaboration between those occupied with traditional humanitarian concerns and those with the care of military personnel.

Likewise, the attention to impartiality underscores the importance of attending to harms caused by all sides to a conflict. While the use of weaponry with questionable accuracy (that would fall under the heading of 'explosive weapons') by pro-Gaddafi forces in populated areas during the war in Libya was widely condemned, opposition fighters also employed such tactics. This also merited concern.[44]

Thinking in terms of public-health-type framing could also be useful in pressing some to undertake novel actions. So overall such a framing emphasizes the importance of identifying the factors that increase or decrease risk. Protective interventions can then be devised. In relation to explosive weapons that might mean, for instance, that before and during armed conflict states should explain the conditions under which the use of explosive weapons in populated areas would be deemed as justified. They should also elaborate on how regard for the local population will be exercised.

Humanitarian organizations could endeavor to supply materials to those deemed at risk in order to enable them to protect themselves (for instance, by putting plastic sheeting for windows). It would further be necessary to provide and evaluate assistance to those affected. Those in a position to help (including belligerent nations) would need to undertake practical steps to measure the impacts of explosive weapons and respond to those affected.[45]

As a point of caution, directing attention to explosive weapons at the level of the use of force could elevate (or at least give special treatment to) a certain type of suffering. In one respect that is exactly the function that frames are meant to fulfill. Yet, to single out particular groups within the context of conflict might well be questionable. For example, with the level of regard given to landmines in the last decade, the plight of survivors from them has received much airing. International agencies involved in what is called 'victim assistance' though, have sought to devise support programs that are not only part of wider violence and disability programs, but are also accessible to all those who need them regardless of the cause of their need.[46]

Just how much the call – central in public-health framings – to collect data and identify risk factors should be linked to specific types of victims and survivors is one question that needs addressing.[47] The suggestion has been forwarded, for example, to concentrate some campaigning attention on children as victims.[48] Assessments of the appropriateness of such efforts will likely depend on assessments of the purposes being served. Some might argue that efforts with regard to explosive weapons could be judged in relation to how much they heighten attention to the harms of armed conflict more widely, whereas others might find this expanding out inappropriate.[49,50]

As another area of possible tension related to purpose, the previous section referred to the central place of systematic evidence in public-health approaches. While evidence is fundamental to identifying a problem, factual claims can also sit uneasily with attempts to persuade people that a problem is a priority. The academic literature on framing suggests that the power to promote a certain understanding of events derives from how it resonates with core values, cultural beliefs, and large-scale frames in society. For instance, whether or not individuals subscribe to the theory that crime rates are primarily caused by blocked opportunities or because of a faulty justice system is not largely driven by detailed evidence about the profile of offenders. Claims of percentages and factors do not necessarily make for compelling arguments. Rather, much depends on how what is known aligns with wider beliefs.

This situation poses a challenge for those thinking about public-health framings that place a great store in systematic evidence. Such evidence may not be effective, or it may even undermine recognition of the category of explosive weapons if it distracts from the core messages. Numbers might well have to make way, at least for many audiences.

This has implications for the ways in which explosive weapons get characterized. Earlier in this chapter, two different kinds of pattern were presented with these weapons: their profile of injuries, and the widespread conventions related to whether or not they are used. While both of these relate to basic values of responsibility and prevention, the latter might well be more amenable to public communication. This is because it is not reliant on audiences taking on board detailed facts and figures. The message is one of double standards rather than comparative percentages. Whether being an easier message to convey makes it the right message is another question.

The two approaches above are also aligned with different kinds of research agendas. Attention to double standards could be documented by putting rules of engagement for the use of force, as well as the licensing and export laws for explosives, side-by-side. A key aim of research would be to identify ways to stigmatize forms of duplicitous behavior. Attention to comparative percentages, in contrast, requires gathering evidence about the effects of different forms of violence in situations of conflict in order to identify relative harms. That might well require finding ways of empowering affected populations to protect themselves and rebuild after conflict.

As another point of concern with public-health framings, it can be said that these have a complex relation to moral condemnations. With the attention to identifying risk factors and seeking practical ways of reducing harm, a potential danger is that of losing sight of moral standards. At issue here is whether the use of explosive weapons in populated areas needs be condemned because of its effects on peoples' health and material standing, or because it is unjust. As a thought experiment, for instance, we might ask how to assess the invasion of a country with such force if that ultimately led to better long-term health services and health outcomes for civilian populations.

That public-health framings are not necessarily well suited to the language of 'right and wrong'[51] can be seen with regard to prohibitions. While these might sometimes be justified through public-health appeals, attention is often directed at undertaking practical steps that minimize harms. The distribution of clean needles to drug addicts is the type of pragmatic step that would be much more readily endorsed in a public-health framing than one built on compliance with the law. As a result, the desire to take whatever practical steps are possible to reduce harm does not necessarily sit easily with trying to stigmatize or ban.

As a final point of consideration, the relation between frames and audiences can be taken one step further. In the manner that a frame offers a particular way of seeing, it is likely to appeal to some over others. Take climate change. Whether this is presented as a looming ecological disaster and an opportunity for new green industries, or as a demand for stewardship of God's earth, matters in relation to who regards it as a legitimate concern.[52] With explosive weapons, public-health framings might or might not appeal to certain audiences.

To what extent framing should be driven by the likely receptiveness of audiences is a moot question. It would be possible, for instance, to imagine alternative portrayals of explosive weapons circulating between military officers, humanitarian NGOs, health professionals, journalists, and so on. For those in the military, for instance, the language and logic of the argument could build on existing operational concepts such as munitions' 'danger zones'. Tailoring the messages presented in order to ensure that they resonant for each group would be one way of building wide-ranging engagement with the category. While this diversity need not imply incompatibility, it can invite suspicions of incoherence and opportunism. Moreover, whether that diversity of understanding can be melded together one day in order to take coherent joint action is another question.

As suggested then, the assessment of the 'fit of frames' depends on an assessment of the issues at hand, the purposes sought, and the next questions to be asked.

Conclusion: Pulling Back

This book has examined organized state violence. Two questions have been posed throughout: How can this be understood and how can it be challenged? Attention has been directed largely at Western governments that speak with a language of regret in using force. Deaths to those not engaged in combat are said to be due to tragic accident, coincidence, or mishap. *How to Look Good in a War* has scrutinized such claims and found them wanting on numerous counts. For major areas of concern, states have been judged as falling well short of upholding the image they publicly trumpet for themselves.

Central to this conclusion has been a rethinking of the terms commonly associated with the study of statecraft: transparency, secrecy, disclosure, concealment, knowledge, and ignorance. That reconsideration, in turn, has facilitated a questioning of the assumptions and preoccupations that often guide studies.

Frequently, attempts to assess warcrafting take it as their purpose to unearth the true but hidden order. The film *The War You Don't See*, directed by journalist John Pilger, represents one such effort to counter lies, dispel illusions, and expose hypocrisy. While admirable in many respects, a contention of this book is that the black-and-white contrasts that motor such critiques work against acknowledging the many subtle ways in which the legitimacy of force gets negotiated.

Instead of conceiving of itself as straightforwardly bringing the buried into the light, *How to Look Good in a War* has taken the study of statecraft to be troubled and troubling. Instead of advancing a definite assessment about what is really propaganda and what is actually factual, it has stepped back to consider what counts as propaganda or 'the facts' from the point of view of how these assessments become established. Instead of simply exposing secrets, it has examined how claims to hidden knowledge are marshaled in consequential ways.

With this set of orientations, I have attempted to suspend initial judgment on the merits of notional moves for transparency, secrecy, disclosure, concealment, knowledge, and ignorance. Transparency and disclosure, for instance, should not be held as necessarily laudable. As contended through the examination in Chapter 1, of official inquiries into distortion of intelligence about Iraqi WMD capabilities, the release of information need not result in greater clarity in political debate, comprehension about what took place, or accountability in decision-making.

The suspension of judgment, in part, derived from recognition of how deftly attempts to disclose, know, and be open shift into acts that censure, ignore, and hide away. As argued throughout this book, this movement is readily possible because the pairings of disclosure–concealment, knowledge–ignorance, and transparency–secrecy do not refer to stark opposites. I have aimed to consider the many dimensions of their interrelation through the cases examined. Extensive disclosure – as in the release of confidential reports – can function to conceal some matters by diverting attention or even by putting them in plain sight.

Instead of relying on ready-to-hand assumptions, what is required then is attentiveness to the specifics of each situation. Attempts to declare once and for all what some action amounted to – whether it was either a bid to further transparency or secrecy – need to give way to an orientation receptive to the past and future unfolding of events.

This book has promoted counter-intuitive ways of thinking in order to cultivate a supple mindfulness for tracking the practices of statecraft. Through this, I hoped to resist hastily imposing labels on actions – political statements, the release of documents, etc. – as being either about 'restriction' or 'openness'. It is inappropriate to regard such actions as discrete objects with some essential nature, as what they amount to must be assessed in relation to the wider negotiation of knowledge dynamics that they are part of. In the ways that disclosure can amount to non-disclosure or ignorance is studiously learned, we need to attend to the fissures formed from the reverberating oscillations of openness and closure in statecraft.

In addition, I have asked how those fissures might be a resource for understanding. So, rather than leaving the examination of the ban on cluster munitions to the more conventional analysis given in Chapter 3, the conversation of Chapter 4 went further. It did so by attending to: (a) how the agreement of a ban on cluster munitions was bound up with the skillful management of information; and (b) how the analysis presented in this chapter of that negotiation itself entailed managed disclosure. Through the first step I wanted to suggest the complex movements and interpersonal dynamics associated with the formation of international treaties that are typically sidelined in scholarly texts. Through the second step I wanted to use a style of writing that encouraged a mindset befitting the study of diplomacy: one in which deliberate attention is dedicated to asking what is absent. Those absences related to matters that were not known, not easy to tell, and for other reasons not mentioned.

A recurring caution raised in *How to Look Good in a War* has been that of overestimating what one has within one's grasp. Whether because of concerns about the deliberate obfuscation or the slipperiness of language, as we attempt to make sense of statecraft regard should be given to the limitations of what is apprehended. Those wishing to suggest that some people are trying to produce a strategic ignorance, for instance, can end up employing many of the same argumentative techniques that they deplore elsewhere: brushing over the ambiguities of words, selectively focusing on certain statements, making questionable presumptions in order to assign meaning, investing groups with an unfounded coherence, and offering definite claims in conditions of partial knowledge.

Chapter 1 provided another caution with grasping too tightly. As contended, it was through the many, varied, and sometimes contradictory ways in which individuals argued about whether or not WMD intelligence had been 'spun' that conditioned the legitimacy accorded to governmental representations of intelligence. As individuals advanced claims about what counted as distortion without much (if any) attention to: (a) how these evaluations were supported; (b) how others were drawing opposing conclusions; or even (c) how specific individuals offered multiple types of evaluations; the basis for claims about whether the intelligence was politicized became locked away from scrutiny. This dynamic, often accompanied by commentators claiming some unique basis for insight, meant that debates about spin descended into a deluge of self-sealing charges and counter-charges in which there was little hope of moving towards agreement – this because there was little scope for questioning the reasoning underpinning evaluations. Indeed, especially because of the many ways in which the faithfulness of intelligence was handled, multiple truths flourished about what the Butler Report reportedly demonstrated.

One lesson drawn from this particular case is the importance of attending to how claims about statecraft are established. All too easily, in relation to this topic, attention can become fixated on the 'whats': what is missing, what is not said, etc. As Lochrie warned in a study of medieval secret-keeping, 'one of the dangers of secrecy is to call our attention to the supposed secrets as the locus of truth, rather than to the operations that make them appear to be truths and the social relationships that are negotiated through them'.[1] *How to Look Good in a War* has sought to examine both the content of 'secrets' kept as well as what the relations of secret-keeping promote – in other words, both objects and processes.

Along these lines, and in keeping with longstanding approaches in fields such as international relations, 'the state' has not been solely conceived of in terms of the working of ministries, departments, civil servants, or elected representatives. Instead, it has been treated as a set of processes that produce and reproduce social orderings, hierarchies, and identities. The management of information was part of providing ready made refutes to critiques of the use of force, perpetuating a belief that organizations were unified, as well as building up certain individuals as being highly competent and erudite (and – sometimes simultaneously – as incompetent and unlearned). Herein, appeals to privy information were prevalent.

With the overall orientation outlined above, in this book I have sought a certain kind of understanding: not the truth of locked-down universal certainty, but rather a modest pragmatic knowledge that seeks to make complex situations intelligible in order to find a way of improving them.[2]

That has meant de-emphasizing certain issues relative to similar studies of war and legitimacy. So the high drama of statecraft is ripe for making allegations that some are deliberately seeking to dissimulate, feign, veil, obfuscate, deceive, disguise, or cover. Agents of the state – such as civil servants or political leaders – are widely held as being able to speak both with exacting precision and with dense ambiguity depending on what is demanded of them. Attributing secreted intent, logics, and rationales to officials provides a way to cohere confused or uncertain events together in order to make a case for underlining obscured and obscuring machinations.[3]

As argued in relation to Chapters 1 and 2, for instance, offering a 'decoding' of the motivations that lay behind the actions of prominent individuals is a frequent move in attempts to sort out what is really going on. It is a move that often becomes dubious because of the temptations of misjudging what is grasped.

The dangers associated with grasping are not simply those of inflating the foresight of, the unity between, and the institutional machinery behind, politicians, civil servants, members of inquires, and others – although this surely is one hazard. Instead, as developed in Chapters 1 and 2, once underlying intent is sought, it is all too easy to blot out variations and inconsistencies in a manner that delimits our vision.

In the case of the inquiry into WMD led by Lord Butler, for instance, the failure to acknowledge how he treated matters of distortion and faithfulness – as *both* resolved and deferred, publicly demonstrated and beyond simple verification, knowable and undecidable, as well as unmistakable and choices of personal preference – meant that attempts by journalists, political pundits, and academics to decipher his real thinking missed the fractured dynamics of how resemblance was established that propelled debates. The many attempts to decode, without acknowledging the varied ways in which decoding were (and were not) being carried out, helped to constitute the restrictive bounds on what was said regarding whether intelligence had been spun. As suggested earlier, they were also part and parcel of how relations of expertise, identity, and hierarchy were produced. Individual decodings by Lord Butler and political commentators were inextricably tied to notions of who was in 'the know' and who was not, and therefore who was credible and who was not. The manner in which the terms of debate enabled many prominent commentators to make a claim for their own (elevated) position of insight meant it helped promote their status.

The stifling implications associated with the smoothing over of rough ground, by attributing secreted motives, was also illustrated in relation to debates about the number of deaths associated with the invasion of Iraq. As argued in Chapter 2, it was not a claim to hidden facts or expert insight that was central to the moral and political legitimacy of governments (in)actions. Instead, it was claims to ignorance. Similarly to the issues covered in Chapter 1, multiple characterizations of what was (not) understood were offered over time. It was through the *combination* of these characterizations that claims about the adequacy of the British and Iraqi governments' regard for the humanitarian consequences of the invasion were supported. The shifting ways in which the British government did and did not portray the Iraqi government as in a position to reliably gauge deaths was also part of identity formation: the building of Iraq as a state in charge of its affairs (rather than then being a shameful proxy for the occupying nations) and responsive to the plight of its citizens.

In line with frequent moves in public debate, the access I gained to correspondence through the Freedom of Information Act could have been deployed as a wedge for splitting through the mutating and tangled claims about what could be known. It would have been possible to marshal that information to make the charge that the UK willfully worked to produce ignorance about deaths. In other words, it was not simply the case that the UK did not know, could not know, or had its eyes shut to Iraqi deaths, but instead that it actively undermined efforts to establish how many people died. As I maintained in Chapter 2, while supported by some evidence, in its stark form this charge could only be advanced by simplifying the events and materials. This would have been particularly open to question because of the unfolding complexity and uncertainty about what was even being discussed. Although there was much discussion about 'reliable death figures', there was seemingly little to no agreement about what 'reliable' meant. Without attending to such considerations, those examining ignorance are at risk of perpetuating it through taking for granted the terms of debate they are studying.

Attending to variations, inconsistencies, and gaps in statecraft as part of striving for a pragmatic understanding was part of how this book shifted away from addressing the question 'What has been revealed?' to the one of 'What alternatives for intervention are possible?'. Along these lines, in Chapters 3 and 4 the fear that the logic of international humanitarian law (IHL) served international complacency inspired novel types of engagement. In outlining how progressive governments, NGOs, and others moved away from the confines of IHL in order to make states' understanding of their use of force into a topic for dispute, these chapters demonstrated how different forms of intervention can help to construct new relations and achievements. The Oslo Process to ban 'unacceptable' cluster munitions challenged many of the traditional ways of handling the rights and wrongs of conflict. In doing so, the lure associated with the past flaunting of 'state secrets' was rendered ineffectual.

Through its questioning of the Oslo Process, Chapter 4 also questioned the commitments and fallibility of the lessons learnt from that process, as well as how efforts to advance humanitarian aims can promote conditions that work against intended aims. The dialogue suggested the dynamic manner in which reappraisals of understanding can lead to new possibilities for action that, in turn, can promote novel understanding. In not simply siding with 'transparency', the chapter was able to recognize many of the troubles and possibilities associated with managed disclosure.

As part of developing revisable and intervention-orientated knowledge, much of Part II took inspiration from the analogy of a conversation. So not only was a dialogue presented in Chapter 4, but interventions to enhance the political accountability of force were likened to turns in conversations.

And as with conversations in general, those considered in this book are infused with hierarchies and conventions. Take the topic of cluster munitions. For decades humanitarian organizations, and others, had raised concerns about their consequences for civilian populations. In turn, stockpiler nations rebuked such worries with unsubstantiated allusions to military requirements and humanitarian heed. In an effort to test what evidence lay behind such claims, some of us sought ways of flipping the ordering of speaking. Rather than those concerned with humanitarian effects 'going first' in making their case, we sought to marshal the history and patterns of concerns to justify that those wishing to retain cluster munitions to make the case first for doing so. The Oslo Process codified this type of approach in its structure for the definition of what should be banned as being a 'cluster munition'. Herein, those wishing to retain weapons were left with the burden of justifying why.

Going second in the debate meant those states opposing continued retention were in the much more advantageous position of picking apart others' justifications. As there was little to no evidence supporting claims about the 'acceptable harm' caused by cluster bombs, this was not a difficult task. Officials from Botswana, Cambodia, Fiji, Guatemala, Zambia, Jamaica, and the Cook Islands frequently and effectively challenged the arguments advanced by major military powers. At its conclusion, the Oslo Process confirmed an assumption that motivated it: that user states had precious little evidence to support their claims that a balance had been struck between 'humanity' and 'military necessity'.

Further extending the conversation analogy, in Chapter 5 different interventions were considered in relation to the impetus they provided for imagination. Strategies were advanced to enable the questioning of what was known about the humanitarian effects of violence as well as promoting discussion of hitherto poorly acknowledged topics. Research into the casualties of war was conceived, in part, as a next turn in an unfolding dialogue. As stressed, it is crucial to attend to the specific purposes sought from any discussion or debate. Whether that is, for instance, to memorialize victims, foster reconciliation, assess operational practice, or measure humanitarian need, matters in determining what information is needed and how it should be regarded.

Such recommendations stand in contrast to the hopelessness attached to death tolls in Chapter 3. The case of Iraq is hardly unique though. The contention that 'we may never know' is rife in public and academic discussions,[4] as in the case of the 2011 NATO intervention in Libya.[5] Contrasting totals get cited as a way of indicating that confounding confusion and irresolvable doubt exists. In not noting that different deaths were being counted, and in not considering the purposes to be served by estimates, such commentaries not only support the belief that ignorance and disagreement are inevitable. They also foster ignorance about how a belief in ignorance gets produced.

A related twin to the suggestion that we cannot know, is the contention that the issues associated with conflict are simply too politicized, morally charged, and inherently disputable to be able to be addressed. Such an orientation results in little more than a reflection on the pathologies of what is claimed to be known.[6] Instead of arguing that deaths from conflict are simply determinable, indeterminable, or politicized, in *How to Look Good in a War* I have sought means of questioning the commitments of our interventions. That has meant not latching onto or pushing away numbers such as '654,965 deaths', but finding ways to hold them at arm's length and to reflect on how they are given meaning.

Alternative ways of talking – of naming the world – were sought in Chapter 6 to transform the possibilities for understanding and action. In recognition of the ways in which our categories of thought are not natural or pre-given, this chapter asked how the grouping 'explosive weapons' could both build on and question existing conventions. At the time of writing this book, this is a category that is snowballing in prominence by means of a dialogue feeding back on itself. NGOs and concerned others have been drawing attention to explosive weapons and seeking a response to the concerns voiced. Some governments and international organizations, in turn, have adopted this language and funded preliminary research. This language and research is now being cited back to concerned (and as yet unconcerned) governments in an effort to shore up the category, identify what is not known, justify further research agendas, and demand action. Subsequent uses of the term, the identification of knowledge 'gaps', research findings, and calls for action will likewise promote future discussions that build the debate further.

As with all types of conversations, those considered in this book need to be understood as being infused with silences. However, these silences do not amount to the mere absences or vacant gaps in dialogue, because for absences and gaps to be noted as silences requires that meaning be imparted to them. For years, governments left their supposed evidence regarding the humanitarian effects of cluster munitions unspoken. It took the Oslo Process to turn that lack of elaboration into a widely noticeable silence. In the negotiating rooms of Dublin, Oslo, Wellington, Vienna, and Lima, the muteness of many governments provided the silent backdrop against which evidence of harms become voluminous.

The importance of attending to the implications of silences and gaps was extended in Chapter 4. In this, an aim was not to glorify or bemoan deliberate concealment, but to attend to what is accomplished by it. Through the combination of what was and was not given, the present absences in the conversation were intended to highlight the need for an orientation of skeptical questioning in making sense of what gets said about statecraft. Rather than a definite history, what was presented was an immersion into a type of active engagement with pregnant unknowns, unspokens, and uncertainties. In this case one that – through its very limitations – spoke to the experience of diplomacy, and in particular how silences and secrets are socially and collaboratively produced. A positive dimension was sought for intentionally limited disclosure. While a conversation format is not necessary for such delicate treading, the expectations for what would be included within conversational banter (a lack of exhaustive elaborations, varying levels of details, threads of thought begun but not followed through, etc.) was in line with the playful partiality of description sought.

As elsewhere, this sort of unconventional format should be judged in relation to what inroads and possibilities it helps foster. And yet, while holding to this, throughout *How to Look Good in a War* a spirit of sensitivity, vigilance, and mindfulness has been sought after in relation to identified inroads and possibilities. This has derived from a view that setting limits to the conduct of war is often tension-ridden. While Chapter 6 highlighted how recent preoccupations and standards for assessing conflict have and have not worked to render the use of explosive weapons in populated areas 'ordinary', it also attended to the choices and binds of promoting alternative ways of categorizing the world.

In other words, what has been sought is a meditative orientation, in the sense of attuning to the implications of our thinking and practices. In a negative sense, that has meant refraining from grasping for certainty about many matters, since doing so can make our understanding and intervention less skillful and generative. In a positive sense, that has meant cultivating an attitude toward statecraft that opens up to new choices and opportunities. Rather than approaching the questions of how to understand and intervene into statecraft as matters with an end resolution, we need approaches that are supple enough to be responsive to the potential for the ever-unfolding of events and relations.

Notes

INTRODUCTION: GRASPING SHADOWS

1. Straw, J. (2004) 'Iraq', *House of Commons – Hansard*, 17 November: column 94WS.
2. Although by no means was this the first intervention that drew critical attention to the issue of civilian deaths. Others included the work of the NGO and Iraq Body Count and Boyce, G. (2004) 'Doomed to Failure in the Middle East', *Guardian*, 27 April.
3. Ibid.
4. Levidow, L. (2001) 'Precautionary Uncertainty: Regulating GM Crops in Europe', *Social Studies of Science*, (31) 6: 842–74.
5. Smithson, M. (1989) *Ignorance and Uncertainty* (New York: Springer-Verlag).
6. Vattimo, G. (1992) *The Transparent Society* (Cambridge: Polity Press).
7. Whitehead, A.N. (1933) *Adventures in Ideas*, New York: Macmillan: 54.
8. Proctor, R. (2008) 'Agnotology: A Missing Term', in R. Proctor and L. Schiebinger (eds.) *Agnotology* (Stanford, CA: Stanford University Press).
9. A theme explored in considerable detail in relation to freedom and constraint in Fish, S. (1994) *There's No Such Thing as Free Speech and it's a Good Thing, Too* (Oxford: Oxford University Press).
10. Rockel, S. and R. Halpern (2009) 'Preface', in S. Rockel and R. Halpern (eds.) *Inventing Collateral Damage* (Toronto: Between the Lines): viii.
11. See Bok, S. (1989) *Secrets* (New York: Vintage); Shils, E. (1956) *The Torment of Secrecy* (Glencoe, IL: Free Press); and Kelly, A. (2002) *The Psychology of Secrets* (London: Kluwer).
12. Khan, R.Y. (2008) *Self and Secrecy in Early Islam* (Columbia, SC: University of South Carolina).
13. Portuondo, M. (2009) *Secret Science* (London: University of Chicago); Morland, H. (2009 [1979]) 'The H-bomb Secret', in S. Marget and J. Goldman (eds.) *Government Secrecy* (London: Libraries Unlimited): 346–59; and Roland, A. (1992) 'Secrecy, Technology, and War: Greek Fire and the Defense of Byzantium, 678–1204', *Technology and Culture*, 33(4): 655–79.
14. Ponting, C. (1990) *Secrecy in Britain* (London: Basil Blackwell); and Rogers, A. (1997) *Secrecy and Power in the British State* (London: Pluto).
15. Vincent, D. (1998) *The Culture of Secrecy* (Oxford: Oxford University Press).
16. As epitomized by the framing of the debate in Goldfarb, R. (2009). *In Confidence* (London: Yale); and Piotrowski, S. (2010) *Transparency and Secrecy* (Lanham, MY: Lexington): Chapter 2.
17. See Ibid: Chapter 2; and Roberts, A. (2006) *Blacked Out* (Cambridge: Cambridge University Press).
18. Hutchings, R. (1987) *Soviet Secrecy and Non-secrecy* (London: MacMillian).
19. And the topics of this book are hardly the only areas where this happens. See, for example, McBarnet, D. (1991) 'Whiter Than White Collar Crime: Tax

Fraud, Insurance and the Management of Stigma', *British Journal of Sociology,* 42: 323–44.

20. In Kipling, R. (1915) *Gehazi,* quoted from Owen, D. (2004) 'How to Read the Butler Report', *The Times* July 17.

21. Rappert, B. and B. Balmer (2007) 'Rethinking "Secrecy" and "Disclosure": What Science and Technology Studies Can Offer Attempts to Governing WMD Threats', in B. Rappert (ed.) *Technology and Security* (London: Palgrave): 45–65.

22. As developed by Simmel, G. (1906), 'The Sociology of Secrecy and of Secret Societies', *American Journal of Sociology,* 11: 441–98.

23. See Gunn, J. (2005) *Modern Occult Rhetoric* (Tuscaloosa, AL: University of Alabama Press) and Rodriguez, N. and A. Ryave, (1992) 'The Structural Organization and Micropolitics of Everyday Secret Telling Interactions', *Qualitative Sociology,* 15(3): 297–318.

24. Teeuwen, M. (2006) 'Introduction' in B. Scheid and M. Teeuwen (eds.) *The Culture of Secrecy in Japanese Religion* (London: Routledge): 1–34.

25. Aftergood, S. and T. Blanton. (1999) 'The Securocrats' Revenge', in S. Marget and J. Goldman (eds.) *Government Secrecy* (London: Libraries Unlimited): 457–59.

26. Balmer, B. (2006) 'A Secret Formula, a Rogue Patent and Public Knowledge About Nerve Gas', *Social Studies of Science,* 36(5): 691–722.

27. Gusterson, H. (1998) *Nuclear Rite* (Berkeley: University of California Press).

28. Dennis, M.A. (1999) 'Secrecy and Science Revisited: From Politics to Historical Practice and Back', in J. Reppy (ed.) *Secrecy and Knowledge Production* (Ithaca: Cornell University Peace Studies).

29. See as well Masco, J. (2001) 'Lie Detectors: Of Secrets and Hypersecurity in Los Alamos' *Public Culture* 14: 441–67; Rappert, B. and B. Balmer. (2007) 'Rethinking "Secrecy" and "Disclosure"', in B. Rappert (ed.) *Technology and Security* (London: Palgrave): 45–65, and Reppy, J. (ed.) (1999) *Secrecy and Knowledge Production* (Ithaca: Cornell University Peace Studies).

30. Much of the analytical work along these lines is from anthropologists concerned with culture, ritual, and initiation. See Bellmen, B. (1981) 'The Paradox of Secrecy' *Human Studies* 4: 1–24; Bellmen, B. (1984) *The Language of Secrecy* (New Brunswick: Rutgers); De Jong, F. (2007) *Masquerades of Modernity* (Edinburgh: Edinburgh University Press); Taussig, M. (1999) *Defacement: Public Secrecy and the Labour of the Negative* (Stanford, CA: Stanford University Press).

31. See Teeuwen, M. (2006) 'Knowing vs. Owning a Secret' in B. Scheid and M. Teeuwen (eds.) *The Culture of Secrecy in Japanese Religion* (London: Routledge): 174–203.

32. Paglen, T. (2009) *Blank Spaces* (New York: Dutton): 17. See also Manguel, A. (1995) 'Daring to Speak One's Name', *Index on Censorship* 24(1): 16–29.

33. For a consideration of such 'secretism' in religion, see Johnson, P.C. (2002) *Secrets, Gossip and Gods* (Oxford: Oxford University Press). As such, classification is not necessarily well conceived of as the non-transmission of information; as in Galison, P. (2004) 'Removing Knowledge', *Critical Inquiry,* 31(1): 229–43.

34. Mookherjee, N. (2006) 'Remembering to Forget: Public Secrecy and Memory of Sexual Violence in the Bangladesh War of 1971', *Journal of the Royal Anthropological Institute,* 12: 433–50.

35. As in Adams, G. and D. Balfour (2011) '"Open Secrets": The Masked Dynamics of Ethical Failures and Administrative Evil' in S. Maret (ed.) *Government Secrecy* (*Research in Social Problems and Public Policy*, Volume 19) (London: Emerald): 403–19.

36. See, for instance, Orszag, P. (2009) *Memorandum for the Heads of Executive Departments and Agencies* – Open Government Directive 8 December (Washington, DC: Executive Office of the President). For an evaluation of such directives see McDermott, P. (2011) 'Secrecy Reform or Secrecy Redux? Access to Information in the Obama Administration' in S. Maret (ed.) *Government Secrecy* (*Research in Social Problems and Public Policy*, Volume 19) (London: Emerald): 189–217.

37. Florini, A. (2003) *The Coming Democracy* (Washington: Island Press): 34. Quoted from Garsten, C. and F. den Hond (2009) 'Hide and Seek': Transparency, Opacity, and the Shadow Side of Accountability in CSR', paper presented at the 25th EGOS Colloquium (Barcelona) July 2: 2.

38. For varied arguments along these lines, Wasserstein, B. (2001) 'Joys and Frustrations of FOIA', *Twentieth Century British History*, (1): 95–105; Roberts, A. (2006) 'Dashed Expectations: Government Adaption to Transparency Rules', in C. Hood and D. Heald (eds.) *Transparency: The Key to Better Governance?* (Oxford: Oxford University Press): 107–25; and Christensen, L.T. and R. Langer (2005) 'Public Relations and the Strategic Use of Transparency', in R.L. Heath, E. Toth and D. Waymer (eds.) *Rhetorical and Critical Approaches to Public Relations II* (London: Routledge): 129–53.

39. Fung, A., M. Graham and D. Weil (2007) *Full Disclosure: The Perils and Promise of Transparency* (Cambridge: Cambridge University Press); and O'Neill, O. (2006) 'Transparency and the Ethics of Communication', in C. Hood and D. Heald (eds.) *Transparency: The Key to Better Governance?* (Oxford: Oxford University Press): 75–90.

40. See, for instance, McBarnet, D. (1991) 'Whiter Than White Collar Crime: Tax, Fraud Insurance and the Management of Stigma', *The British Journal of Sociology*, 42(3): 323–44. It should be noted that this outcome need not result from intentional deception, as any openness has its end.

41. Stavrianakis, A. (2010) *Taking Aim at the Arms Trade* (London: Zed): 10.

42. Proctor, R. (2008) 'Agnotology: A Missing Term', in R. Proctor and L. Schiebinger (eds.) *Agnotology* (Stanford, CA: Stanford University Press); Gladwell, M. (2007) 'Enron, Intelligence, and the Perils of Too Much Information' *The New Yorker* 82(44). Available at: www.newyorker.com/reporting/2007/01/08/070108fa_fact_gladwell. Accessed on April 22, 2011; and Easton, M. (2010) 'Whitehall Spending: Information Overload', *BBC News*, November 19.

43. Roberts, A. (2006) 'Dashed Expectations: Government Adaption to Transparency Rules', in C. Hood and D. Heald (eds.) *Transparency: The Key to Better Governance?* (Oxford: Oxford University Press): 107–25.

44. Christensen, L.T. (2002) 'Corporate Communication: The Challenge of Transparency', *Corporate Communication* 7(3): 162–8.

45. Christensen, L.T. and R. Langer (2005) 'Public Relations and the Strategic Use of Transparency' in R.L. Heath, E. Toth and D. Waymer (eds.) *Rhetorical and Critical Approaches to Public Relations II* (London: Routledge): 129–53; and Vattimo, G. (1992) *The Transparent Society* (Cambridge: Polity Press).

46. Power, M. (1997) *The Audit Society* (Oxford: Oxford University Press): 127.

47. See Maret, S. (2009) 'Introduction', in S. Marget and J. Goldman (eds.) *Government Secrecy* (London: Libraries Unlimited): xvii–xxv; and Robertson, K.G. (1999) *Secrecy and Open Government* (London: Macmillan).
48. Rappert, B. (2010) 'Revealing and Concealing Secrets in Research: The Potential for the Absent', Qualitative Research 10(5): 571–588; and Gunn, J. (2005) *Modern Occult Rhetoric* (Tuscaloosa: University of Alabama Press).
49. Gunn, J. (2005) *Modern Occult Rhetoric* (Tuscaloosa: University of Alabama Press).
50. This theme is explored in great length in Johnson, P.C. (2002) *Secrets, Gossip and Gods* (Oxford: Oxford University Press).
51. Taking inspiration from Dewey, J. (1929) *The Quest for Certainty* (London: George Allen & Unwin).
52. Taussig, M. (2003) 'Viscerality, faith, and skepticism', in B. Meyer and P. Pels (eds.) *Magic and Modernity* (Stanford, CA: Stanford University Press): 305.

1   SHOW AND TELL: DISTORTION, CONCEALMENT, AND WMD

1. Blair, T. (2002) in *Iraq's Weapons of Mass Destruction: The Assessment of the British Government*, September 24 (London: Stationery Office). Available at: www.fco.gov.uk/resources/en/pdf/pdf3/fco_iraqdossier. Date last accessed: February 20, 2011.
2. For a consideration of what makes WMD 'WMD', see Rappert, B. (2006) *Controlling the Weapons of War* (London: Routledge): Chapter 6.
3. For a history of UN inspections in Iraq see Blix, H. (2004) *Disarming Iraq* (London: Pantheon); and Ritter, S. (2006) *Iraq Confidential: The Untold Story of the Intelligence Conspiracy to Undermine the UN and Overthrow Saddam Hussein* (New York: Nation Books).
4. No. 10 Downing Street (2002) *Iraq's Weapons of Mass Destruction: The Assessment of the British Government*, 24 September (London: Stationery Office); and CIA. (2002) *The National Intelligence Estimate: Iraq's Continuing Programs for Weapons of Mass Destruction* (Langley: CIA).
5. Gusterson, H. (2005) 'The Auditors: Bad Intelligence and the Loss of Public Trust', *Boston Review,* November/December. Available at: http://bostonreview.net/BR30.6/gusterson.php. Date last accessed: February 20, 2011.
6. Ibid.
7. For a conceptual exploration of how the ability to comprehend depends on training, see Teeuwen, M. (2006) 'Knowing vs. Owning a Secret', in B. Scheid and M. Teeuwen (eds.) *The Culture of Secrecy in Japanese Religion* (London: Routledge): 174–203.
8. See Millar, S. (2003) 'Spy in the Sky Good Enough for Most Experts on the Ground', *The Guardian,* February.
9. Dutch committee of inquiry on the war in Iraq (2010) 'Report of the Dutch Committee of Inquiry on the War in Iraq', *Netherlands International Law Review* (LVII): 81–137.
10. US Senate (2004) *Report on the U.S. Intelligence Community's Pre-War Intelligence Assessments,* July 7; Foreign Affairs Committee (2003) *The Decision to go to War in Iraq* (London: HMSO); Intelligence and Security Committee (2003) *Iraqi Weapons of Mass Destruction – Intelligence and Assessments* (London: HMSO); WMD Commission (2005) *Final Report of the Commission on the Intelligence Capabilities of the United States Regarding Weapons of Mass*

Destruction, March 31; Parliamentary Joint Committee on ASIO, ASIS and DSD (2004) *Intelligence on Iraq's Weapons of Mass Destruction* No. 47/2004 (Canberra: Parliament of Australia).

11. See Public Broadcasting Service (2006) 'The Dark Side' FRONTLINE. Available at: www.pbs.org/wgbh/pages/frontline/darkside/view/. Date last accessed: February 20, 2011.

12. For an account of how pre-existing expectations influence how intelligence is understood, see Jackson, P. (2010) 'On Uncertainty and the Limits of Intelligence', in L. Johnson (ed.) *The Oxford Handbook of National Security Intelligence* (Oxford: Oxford University Press): 453.

13. See Boudeau, C. (2007) 'Producing Threat Assessments: An Ethnomethodological Perspective on Intelligence on Iraq's Aluminium Tubes', in B. Rappert (ed.) *Technology and Security* (London: Palgrave); Barron, Peter (2006) 'Interview a Statesman, Design a Set', *BBC Newsnight*, January 20. Available at: http://news.bbc.co.uk/1/hi/programmes/newsnight/4631408.stm. Date last accessed: February 20, 2011; and Leonard, J.W. (2011) 'The Corrupting Influence of Secrecy on National Policy Decisions' in S. Maret (ed.) *Government Secrecy (Research in Social Problems and Public Policy, Volume 19)* (London: Emerald): 421–34.

14. Blair, T. (2002) in *Iraq's Weapons of Mass Destruction: The Assessment of the British Government*, September 24 (London: Stationery Office). Available at: www.fco.gov.uk/resources/en/pdf/pdf3/fco_iraqdossier. Date last accessed: February 20, 2011.

15. Butler, Lord R., Rt. Hon. A. Taylor, Rt. Hon. Sir J. Chilcot, Rt. Hon. M. Mates, Rt. Hon. Field Marshal Lord Inge (2004) *Review of Intelligence on Weapons of Mass Destruction* HC 898 (London: HMSO): 76.

16. Humphreys, J. (2005) 'The Iraq Dossier and the Meaning of Spin', *Parliamentary Affairs*, 58(1): 156–70.

17. Hutton, Lord (2004) *Report of the Inquiry into the Circumstances Surrounding the Death of Dr David Kelly C.M.G. Appendix 3 – Transcript of Telephone Conversation between Ms Susan Watts and Dr Kelly on 30 May 2003* (London: HMSO): 12.

18. For claims about the importance of the dossier, see Coole, D. (2005) 'Agency, Truth and Meaning: Judging the Hutton Report', *British Journal of Political Science,* 35: 465.

19. Ibid.

20. Intelligence and Security Committee (2003) *Iraqi Weapons of Mass Destruction – Intelligence and Assessments* (London: HMSO); and Foreign Affairs Committee (2003) *The Decision to go to War in Iraq* (London: HMSO).

21. See Doig, A. (2005) '45 Minutes of Infamy?', *Parliamentary Affairs*, 58(1): 109–23; Porter, H. (2004) 'Are We All Mad, or Is It Hutton?', *The Observer,* Sunday February 1; Jones, G., T. Leonard and M. Born (2004) 'Hutton a Whitewash, Say 56pc', *Telegraph*, January 30; and Phythian, M. (2005) 'Hutton and Scott: A Tale of Two Inquires', *Parliamentary Affairs*, 58(1): 124–13.

22. For instance, Humphreys downplayed concerns about the pre-publication rewrites proposed by Downing Street officials, see Humphreys, J. (2005) 'The Iraq Dossier and the Meaning of Spin', *Parliamentary Affairs*, 58(1): 156–70.

23. From Appendix 3 of Hutton, Lord (2004) *Report of the Inquiry into the Circumstances Surrounding the Death of Dr David Kelly C.M.G.*

Appendix 3 - Transcript of Telephone Conversation between Ms Susan Watts and Dr Kelly on 30 May 2003 (London: HMSO).

24. Ibid: 152.

25. Goodman, N. (1972) *Problems and Projects* (New York: Bobbs-Merrill Company).

26. Coole, D. (2005) 'Agency, Truth and Meaning: Judging the Hutton Report', *British Journal of Political Science*, 35: 475. For a wider examination of how the politicization of intelligence cannot be reduce to black-and-white distinctions, see Pillar, P. (2010) 'The Perils of Politicization', in L. Johnson *The Oxford Handbook of National Security Intelligence* (Oxford: Oxford University Press): 479–81.

27. Butler, Lord R., Rt. Hon. A. Taylor, Rt. Hon. Sir J. Chilcot, Rt. Hon. M. Mates and Rt. Hon. Field Marshal Lord Inge (2004) *Review of Intelligence on Weapons of Mass Destruction* HC 898 (London: HMSO): 1.

28. See Phythian, M. (2010) 'Flawed Intelligence, Limited Oversight: Official Inquiries into Prewar UK Intelligence on Iraq', in J. Pfiffner and M. Phythian (eds.) *Intelligence and National Security Policy Making in Iraq* (Manchester: Manchester University Press).

29. Although some have argued that the inquiry's report did diminish political support for Labour, see Phythian, M. (2010) 'The British Road to War' in J. Pfiffner and M. Phythian (eds.) *Intelligence and National Security Policy Making in Iraq* (Manchester: Manchester University Press).

30. Pillar, P. (2010) 'Intelligence, Policy and the War in Iraq' in J. Pfiffner and M. Phythian (eds.) *Intelligence and National Security Policy Making in Iraq* (Manchester: Manchester University Press).

31. Specifically, *The Guardian* (and *The Observer*), *The Times* (and *The Sunday Times*), *The Daily Telegraph* (and *The Sunday Telegraph*), *The Independent*, and *The Sun* web archives were searched between July 14, 2004 and January 14, 2005 for the terms 'Butler' and 'report'.

32. Debates, written answers, committee hearings and publications, business papers, and other activities for the UK House of Commons and House of Lords were searched in line with the newspapers.

33. This excluding Lord Butler to House of Commons Select Committee on Public Administration which is referred to separately in this chapter.

34. For a detailed analysis of the layout of this report and how it fosters certain types of interpretations, see Boudeau, C. (2008) *Seeking and Finding Society in the Text*. PhD Dissertation (Uxbridge: Brunel University).

35. This includes references to Annex B columns that are considered later in the chapter.

36. Black, C. (2004) 'A Slow-burn Report to Stop the Rot', *The Guardian,* July 15. Other references included House of Commons statements by Ken Clarke MP (July 14, 2004) and Michael Meacher MP (July 20, 2004) as well as newspaper articles by Jonathan Freedland *The Guardian* (July 15, 2004) and David Owen *The Times* (July 17, 2004).

37. So lamented Symons, Baroness E. (2004) *House of Lords Hansard* , September 7 (London: HMSO): column 548.

38. Other instances of such sentiments were evident in exchanges such as those that took place on July 20, 2004 in the House of Commons.

39. Hennessy, P. (2004) 'The Lightening Flash on the Road to Baghdad', in W.G. Runciman (ed.) *Hutton and Butler: Lifting the Lid on the Workings of Power* (Oxford: Oxford University Press): 73.

40. See Grice, A. (2004) 'The More that I Think about the Butler Report, the More Devastating it Becomes', *The Independent*, July 17; *The Guardian* (2004) 'Lessons Blair Must Learn' *The Guardian*, July 15; Ashley, J. (2004) 'After Butler's Damning Report, He Should Search His Conscience Again', *The Guardian*, July 15; Norman, M. (2004) 'Like Jeeves, this Butler's First Language is Euphemism', *The Guardian*, July17; and Holme, Lord R. (2004) *House of Lords Hansard*, September 7 (London: HMSO): column 478.

41. The Independent (2004) 'How "Patchy" Intelligence Became Proof Saddam Possessed WMD', *The Independent*, July 15.

42. Compare and contrast Davies, C. (2004) 'Mandarin a Maestro of the No-blame Game', *The Daily Telegraph*, July 15; Goodhart, Lord W. (2004) *House of Lords Hansard*, November 29 (London: HMSO): column 356; Anderson, D. (2004) *House of Commons Hansard*, July 20 (London: HMSO): column 256; Beith, A. (2004) *House of Commons Hansard*, July 20 (London: HMSO): column 239.

43. Such efforts at explicit decoding were one of many attempts to justify the conclusion that the report was far more critical than it might appear. As in, for example, Pfiffner, J. and Phythian, M. (2010) 'Introduction', in J. Pfiffner and M. Phythian (eds.) *Intelligence and National Security Policy Making in Iraq* (Manchester: Manchester University Press): 1–15.

44. As he would have no doubt done in relation to readings of the report such as that given in Phythian, M. (2010) 'Flawed Intelligence, Limited Oversight: Official Inquiries into Prewar UK Intelligence on Iraq', in J. Pfiffner and M. Phythian (eds.) *Intelligence and National Security Policy Making in Iraq* (Manchester: Manchester University Press).

45. House of Commons Select Committee on Public Administration (2004) *Government by Inquiry* – Minutes of Evidence October 21 (London: The Stationery Office): Q 495.

46. Butler, Lord R., Rt. Hon. A. Taylor, Rt. Hon. Sir J. Chilcot, Rt. Hon. M. Mates and Rt. Hon. Field Marshal Lord Inge (2004) *Review of Intelligence on Weapons of Mass Destruction* HC 898 (London: HMSO): 79–80.

47. See House of Commons Select Committee on Public Administration (2004) *Government by Inquiry* – Minutes of Evidence October 21 (London: The Stationery Office): Q483, Q460 and Q467.

48. Intelligence and Security Committee (2003) *Iraqi Weapons of Mass Destruction – Intelligence and Assessments* (London: HMSO): para 127.

49. High-level appointed advisors to the British government.

50. House of Commons Select Committee on Public Administration. (2004) *Government by Inquiry* – Minutes of Evidence October 21 (London: The Stationery Office): Q506–7.

51. See as well in this regard, Ibid: Q533–534.

52. For a discussion of secrets, see Kippenberg, H.G. and Stroumsa, G.G. (1995) 'Introduction', in H.G. Kippenberg and G.G Stroumsa (eds.) *Secrecy and Concealment* (Leiden: E.J. Brill).

53. Butler, Lord R., Rt. Hon. A., Taylor, Rt. Hon. Sir J. Chilcot, Rt. Hon. M. Mates and Rt. Hon. Field Marshal Lord Inge (2004) *Review of Intelligence on Weapons of Mass Destruction* HC 898 (London: HMSO): 76.

54. See also Jackson, P. (2010) 'On Uncertainty and the Limits of Intelligence', in L. Johnson (ed.) *The Oxford Handbook of National Security Intelligence* (Oxford: Oxford University Press); and Doig A. and M. Phythian (2005) 'The National Interest and the Politics of Threat Exaggeration', *Political Quarterly*, 76(3): 368–76.

55. Coole, D. (2005) 'Agency, Truth and Meaning: Judging the Hutton Report', *British Journal of Political Science*, 35: 476.

56. For example, Norton-Taylor, R. (2010) 'Iraq War Inquiry: Blair Government "Massaged" Saddam Hussein WMD Threat', *Guardian*, July 12; Phythian, M. (2010) 'Flawed Intelligence, Limited Oversight: Official Inquiries into Prewar UK Intelligence on Iraq', in J. Pfiffner and M. Phythian (eds.) *Intelligence and National Security Policy Making in Iraq* (Manchester: Manchester University Press): 85–105; and BBC News (2011) 'Iraq Inquiry: Campbell Dossier Evidence Questioned', *BBC News*, May 12. Available at: www.bbc.co.uk/news/uk-politics-13371751. Date last accessed: May 12, 2011. Related to this see Laurie, M. (2010) *Letter to the Iraq Inquiry*, January 27. Available at: www.iraqinquiry.org.uk/media/52051/Laurie-statement-FINAL.pdf. Date last accessed: May 12, 2011.

2   ESTIMATING IGNORANCE

1. For instance, İhsanoğlu, E. (2007) 'Assessing the Human Tragedy in Iraq', *International Review of the Red Cross*, 89 (868): 915–27; and Pfiffner, J. and M. Phythian, (2010) 'Introduction', in J. Pfiffner and M. Phythian (eds.) *Intelligence and National Security Policy Making in Iraq* (Manchester: Manchester University Press): 1–15.

2. Rummel, R. (1994) *Death by Government* (New Brunswick: Transaction).

3. See Schaffer, R. (1985) *Wings of Judgment* (Oxford: Oxford University Press).

4. Grayling, A.C. (2006) *Among the Dead Cities* (London: Bloomsbury): Chapter 2.

5. Garrett, S. (1997) *Ethics and Airpower in World War II* (New York: St Martin's Press): Chapter 1. For a comprehensive survey of these issues see as well Knightley, P. (2004) *The First Casualty: The War Correspondent as Hero and Myth-maker from Crimea to Iraq* (Baltimore, MA: Johns Hopkins University Press).

6. Beach, H., et al (2008) 'Cluster Bombs Don't Work and Must Be Banned', *The Times*, May 19.

7. Leigh, D. (2010) 'Afghanistan War Logs: Secret CIA Paramilitaries' Role in Civilian Deaths', *The Guardian*, July 25.

8. Norton-Taylor, R. (2010) 'Afghanistan War Logs: Shattering the Illusion of a Bloodless Victory', *The Guardian*, July 25.

9. Leigh, D. (2010) 'Afghanistan War Logs: Secret CIA Paramilitaries' Role in Civilian Deaths', *The Guardian*, July 25.

10. The Guardian (2010) 'Afghanistan War Logs: The Unvarnished Picture', *The Guardian*, July 25.

11. Daponte, B.O. (1993) 'A Case Study in Estimating Casualties from War and its Aftermath: The 1991 Persian Gulf War', *Physicians for Social Responsibility Quarterly*, 3:57–66

12. To elaborate, those requests were:

> *Set 1*: In November 2007, Landmine Action (now Action on Armed Violence) asked the Foreign and Commonwealth Office (FCO), Department for International Development (DFID), and Ministry of Defence (MoD) for information since 2001 regarding what projects they had 'funded, undertaken or analysed in a) Afghanistan b) Iraq that work, *inter alia*, to assess the numbers and specific causes of civilian casualties resulting from armed violence perpetrated by UK forces and our relevant international partners?' and what 'analyses or assessments have been made [...] regarding methodologies for assessing the civilian cost of armed violence'.
>
> *Set 2*: In 2009–10, the author wrote to the FCO, DFID, MoD, and Department of Health (DoH) re-asking the 2007 Set 1 questions in relation to Iraq.
>
> *Set 3*: In 2009, a request was made to the FCO by a third party asking for information pertaining to 'the feasibility, accuracy, and results of any assessments made by the UK government of the number of direct and indirect casualties in Iraq' with particular emphasis on a study published in the medical journal The Lancet. The released information was initially withheld, but then later made public following a decision notice issued by the Information Commissioner's Office that resulted from a complaint. It is available at: http://foi.fco.gov.uk/content/en/foi-releases/2009/lancet-report. Date last accessed: February, 20 2011.

13. Wasserstein, B. (2001) 'Joys and Frustrations of FOIA', *Twentieth Century British History,* (1): 95–105.

14. See Hoon, G. (2003) 'Iraq', *Hansard – House of Commons,* (London: HMSO): Column 1087.

15. O'Brien, M. (2003) 'Iraqi civilian deaths', *Hansard – House of Commons,* April 8 (London: HMSO): Column 190W.

16. Ingram, A. (2003) 'Iraq', *Hansard – House of Commons,* April 3 (London: HMSO): Column 783W.

17. See Boyce, G., et al (2004) 'Doomed to Failure in the Middle East', *Guardian,* April 27. Available at: www.guardian.co.uk/politics/2004/apr/27/foreignpolicy.world

18. Ingram, A. (2004) 'Iraq', *House of Commons – Hansard,* June 14 (London: HMSO): Column 642W.

19. Roberts, L., R. Lafta, R. Garfield, J. Khudhairi and G. Burnham, (2004) 'Mortality Before and After the 2003 Invasion of Iraq: Cluster Sample Survey', *Lancet,* 364: 1857–64.

20. Ibid: 1857.

21. See Geneva Declaration Secretariat (2008) *Global Burden of Armed Violence,* June (Geneva: Geneva Declaration Secretariat): Chapter 2.

22. For example, Iraq Body Count, a civil society driven initiative, tabulates news accounts as well as other substantiated reports. According to the UK Government, Iraq Body Count recorded between 14,284 and 16,419 civilians reported to have died directly from military or paramilitary violence from the start of the war to roughly the time of *The Lancet* research.

23. Symons, Baroness (2004) 'Iraq', *House of Lords – Hansard,* June 24 (London: HMSO): column WA138.

24. Symons, Baroness (2004) 'Iraq', *House of Lords – Hansard,* June 7 (London: HMSO): column WA2.

25. International Republican Institute (2004) *Survey of Iraqi Public Opinion* (Washington DC: IRI).

26. Alvesson, M. (2002) *Postmodernism and Social Research* (Buckingham: Open University Press); Lynch, M. and D. Bogen (1996) *The Spectacle of History* (Durham, NC: Duke University Press); and Blommaert, J. (2005) *Discourse* (Cambridge: Cambridge University Press).

27. O'Neill makes another distinct but related argument about how access to information does not always ensure effective communication, because audience do not have the ethical and epistemic capacity to comprehend it. See O'Neill, O. (2006) 'Transparency and the Ethics of Communication', in C. Hood and D. Heald (eds.) *Transparency: The Key to Better Governance*, (Oxford: Oxford University Press): 75–90.

28. Arminen, I. (2000) 'On the Context Sensitivity of Institutional Interaction', *Discourse & Society*, 11(4): 435–58.

29. For an attempt to give that context through claiming access to the inside facts, see Pearce, F. (2010) *The Climate Files* (London: Guardian Books).

30. Gilbert, N. and M. Mulkay (1984) *Opening Pandora's Box* (Cambridge: Cambridge University Press): 2.

31. A non-dated (but post-2004) released Foreign Office analysis of 'African Conflict Statistics' provided detailed grounds for concerns about the reliability of conflict statistics.

32. The names of officials were deemed 'not relevant' by the FCO to the questions posed by Richard Moyes as characterized in Griffiths, R. (2008) *Freedom of Information Request 0873-07*, January 30 (London: Foreign and Commonwealth Office).

33. FCO (2004) *Iraq: Civilian Casualty Figures*, October 14.

34. As did others too. In December 2004, in response to a parliamentary question about whether the UK needed to 'hold an independent inquiry into the number of civilian casualties in Iraq since the invasion' under its international legal obligations, the then Prime Minister Tony Blair rejected the suggestion:

> I do not accept that. In our view the figures from the Iraqi Ministry of Health, which has surveyed the hospitals there, constitute the most accurate survey that there is, but let me just make this point to the hon. Gentleman and, through him, to the authors of the letter today: those who are killing innocent people in Iraq today – those who are responsible for innocent people dying – are the terrorists and insurgents who want to stop the elections happening in Iraq. Any action that the multinational force or the Iraqi army is taking in Iraq is intended to defeat those people, who are blowing up innocent people, preventing people from joining the police force and killing innocent aid workers – killing anyone trying to make the country better.
>
> See Blair, T. (2004) 'Engagements', *House of Commons – Hansard*, December 8 (London: HMSO): Column 1165. This statement addressed other calls at the time to determine the number of civilians killed, such as a letter to the Prime Minister from over 40 individuals including former British military officers and ambassadors, scholars, and religious leaders. See Annex B: 'Demands Grow for Iraq Death Count', *BBC* News, December 8. Available at: http://news.bbc.co.uk/1/hi/uk_politics/4076993.stm. Date last accessed: February 20, 2011.

35. As in Goffman, E. (1970) *Strategic Interaction* (Oxford: Basil Blackwell).

36. Burnham, G., R. Lafta, S. Doocy and L. Roberts, (2006) 'Mortality After the 2003 invasion of Iraq: A Cross-sectional Cluster Sample Survey', *Lancet*, 368: 1421–28.
37. Tempest, M. (2006) 'Beckett Rejects Iraq Death Toll', *Guardian*, October 12.
38. Lord Triesman (2006) 'Iraq: Casualties', *Hansard – House of Lords*, October 19 (London: HMSO): Column 871.
39. In 2010, the MoD released to the author a four-page paper titled 'Analysis of 2006 Lancet Article – Summary of Findings' (undated and without an identified author) that was not cited elsewhere or released as part of the other FoI requests. It likewise judged the methodology sound and (on balance) supported the study's findings.
40. Horton, R. (2007) 'A Monstrous War Crime', *The Guardian*, March 28.
41. Especially in contrast to Jack Straw's 1,600 word statement on November 17, 2004.
42. Lord Triesman (2006) 'Iraq: Casualties', *Hansard – House of Lords*, October 19 (London: HMSO): Column 871.
43. As in Ravetz, J.R. (1987) 'Usable Knowledge, Usable Ignorance', *Science Communication*, (9):87–116.
44. Norris, M. (1994) 'Only the Guns have Eyes', in S. Jeffords and L. Rabinovitz (eds.) *Seeing Through the Media* (New Brunswick, NJ: Rutgers University Press): 290.
45. While it is reasonable to consider that states have a fundamental responsibility to understand the nature and impact of violence amongst their populations, the UK's disavowal of any responsibility in this context is problematic for a number of reasons. Firstly, the 2003 conflict in Iraq, and the violence set in train by that conflict, was directly initiated by the UK and its international partners. In such a situation the UK should also bear a responsibility to understand the impact of that decision.

    Secondly, both the legitimacy of the conflict as a whole and the legitimacy of individual attacks within that conflict may depend on an estimation of 'proportionality' – that the unintended harm to civilians is not excessive in relation to the anticipated benefits. It is not possible to make such estimations if States systematically avoid coming to any understanding of the actual civilian harm caused.

    Thirdly, the Iraqi Government was then facing pressing challenges, not least the levels of ongoing armed violence, and therefore lacked the capacity to meet its responsibilities in this respect beyond the basic levels of hospital and mortuary data.
46. Howells, K. (2007) 'Iraq', *House of Commons – Hansard*, October 9 (London: HMSO): Column 545W.
47. In relation to the latter, it was written that 'No information is given on how the figures are reached. Our embassy in Baghdad thinks they are an average of MOH/MOI/MOD figures, however, all these departments reach their totals in different ways'.
48. Iraq Family Health Survey Study Group (2008) 'Violence-related Mortality in Iraq from 2002 to 2006', New England Journal of Medicine, 358(2): 484–93.
49. With a 95 percent uncertainty range of the estimate being between 104,000 and 223,000.
50. Howells, K. (2007) 'Iraq', *House of Commons – Hansard*, October 9 (London: HMSO): Column 545W.

51. See, for instance, Brown, D. and J. Partlow (2008) 'New Estimate of Violent Deaths Among Iraqis is Lower', *Washington Post,* January 10; Steele, J. and S. Goldenberg (2008) 'What is the Real Death Toll in Iraq?', *Guardian,* March 19; Susman, T. (2007) 'Iraq Won't Give Casualty Figures to U.N.', *Chicago Tribune,* April 26: 12. In addition, the aforementioned 2007 FCO checklist made brief reference to dispute about figures within Iraq.
52. The Iraq Index being based on estimations and counts made by other organisations, including Iraq Body Count.
53. Slim, H. (2007) *Killing Civilians* (London: Hurst & Company): 174.
54. Goffman, E. (1970) *Strategic Interaction* (Oxford: Basil Blackwell).
55. Eisenberg, E. (1984) 'Ambiguity as Strategy in Organizational Communication', *Communication Monographs,* 51: 227–42.
56. Differences which made it difficult for the author to comprehend what legitimate grounds existed for the redacting of material. For instance, the previously cited extract from a letter by a chief economist, had the title of 'chief economist' redacted from only one of the two released copies.
57. Contrast this to BBC (2009) 'Iraq Memos Show Death Toll Unease', *BBC News,* April 29. Available at: http://news.bbc.co.uk/2/hi/uk_news/8025942.stm. Date last accessed: February, 20 2011.
58. Smithson, M. (1993) 'Ignorance and Science', *Science Communication,* 15(2): 133–56.
59. Oreskes, N. and E. Conway (2008) 'Challenging Knowledge', in R. Proctor and L. Schiebinger (eds.) *Agnotology* (Stanford, CA: Stanford University Press): 55–89.
60. As done in Ellis, M. (2009) 'Vital statistics', *Professional Geographer,* 61(3): 301–9.

3   DISABLING DISCOURSES: INTERNATIONAL LAW, LEGITIMACY, AND THE POLITICS OF BALANCE

1. Quote from the 1868 Declaration of St. Petersburg.
2. See Perrigo, S. and J. Whitman (eds.) (2010) *The Geneva Conventions Under Assault* (London: Pluto).
3. See Henckaerts, J.-M. and L. Doswald-Beck (2005) *Customary International Humanitarian Law* (Cambridge: Cambridge University Press).
4. See International Committee of the Red Cross (2005) *Existing Principles and Rules of International Humanitarian Law Applicable to Munitions that May Become Explosive Remnants of War – Paper Submitted to the Convention on Prohibitions or Restrictions on the Use of Certain Conventional Weapons Which May Be Deemed to Be Excessively Injurious or to Have Indiscriminate Effects* CCW/GGE/XI/WG.1/WP.7, July 28.
5. For governments' claims to this effect see 'Statement by Ambassador Bernhard Brasack Permanent Representative of Germany to the Conference on Disarmament "Explosive Remnants of War"' March 8, 2006; and Russia (2005) *Responses to Document CCW/GGE/X/WG.1/WP.2, Entitled IHL and ERW, dated 8 March 2005.* Group of Government Experts of States Parties to the Convention on Prohibitions or Restrictions on the Use of Certain Conventional Weapons Which May Be Deemed to Be Excessively Injurious or to Have Indiscriminate Effects CCW/GGE/XII/WG.1/WP.3 October 21.

6. See McCormick, T., P. Mtharu and S. Finnin (2006) *Report on States Parties' Responses to the Questionnaire March and US/UK, Conduct of the 2003 War in Iraq, Case No. 153: 1600*. Available at: https://portfolio.du.edu/portfolio/getportfoliofile?uid=82266. Date last accessed: February 20, 2011.

7. The Republic of Croatia (2005) *Responses to Document CCW/GGE/X/WG.1/WP.2, Entitled IHL and ERW, dated 8 March 2005*. Group of Government Experts of States Parties to the Convention on Prohibitions or Restrictions on the Use of Certain Conventional Weapons Which May Be Deemed to Be Excessively Injurious or to Have Indiscriminate Effects CCW/GGE/XII/WG.1/WP.7, November 11.

8. United States (2005) *Responses to Document CCW/GGE/XI/WG.1/WP.2, Entitled IHL and ERW, dated 8 March 2005*. Group of Government Experts of States Parties to the Convention on Prohibitions or Restrictions on the Use of Certain Conventional Weapons Which May Be Deemed to Be Excessively Injurious or to Have Indiscriminate Effects CCW/GGE/XI/WG.1/WP.8, July 25: 3.

9. For an extensive analysis of the application of the rules of IHL to another specific technology, see Barak, E. (2011) *Deadly Metal Rain: The Legality of Flechette Weapons in International Law* (Leiden: Martinus Nijhoff Publishers).

10. For example, Human Rights Watch Background Paper (1999) *NATO's Use of Cluster Munitions in Yugoslavia*. Available at: www.hrw.org/backgrounder/arms/clus0511.htm. Date last accessed: February 20, 2011.

11. Human Rights Watch (2000) *Civilian Deaths in the NATO Air Campaign* (New York: HRW).

12. International Committee of the Red Cross (2001) *Explosive Remnants of War* August (Geneva: ICRC).

13. Ibid: 9.

14. See, for instance, Peachey, T. and V. Wiebe (2000) *Clusters of Death* – Chapter 3: Cluster Munitions Use by Russian Federation Forces in Chechnya November (Akron, PA: Mennonite Central Committee).

15. Landmine Monitor (2002) *Landmine Monitor Report 2002* (Geneva: ICBL).

16. Nash, T. (2006) *Foreseeable Harm* (London: Landmine Action).

17. Human Rights Watch (2008) *Flooding South Lebanon* (New York: HRW).

18. UN Human Rights Council (2006) *Implementation of General Assembly Resolution 60/251 of 15 March 2006 Entitled 'Human Rights Council'* – *Mission to Lebanon and Israel* A/HRC/2/7, October 10.

19. Israel Ministry of Foreign Affairs (2006) 'IDF to Probe Use of Cluster Munitions in Lebanon War', November 21. Available at: www.mfa.gov.il/MFA/Government/Communiques/2006/IDF%20to%20probe%20use%20of%20cluster%20munitions%20in%20Lebanon%20War%2021-Nov-2006. Date last accessed: February, 20 2011.

20. Barak, E. (2010) 'None to be Trusted: Israel's Use of Cluster Munitions in the Second Lebanon War and the Case for the Convention on Cluster Munitions', *American University International Law Review* 25(3): 423–83.

21. Gates, R. (2008) *DoD Policy on Cluster Munitions and Unintended Harm to Civilians*, June 19 (Washington, DC: DoD). For another example of this see Hoon, G. (2003) 'Iraq', *House of Commons Hansard*, April 3 (London: HMSO): Column 107. For more historical examples of such claims, see Krepon, M. (1974) 'Weapons Potentially Inhumane', *Foreign Affairs* 52: 595–611.

22. Ibid.

23. Borrie, J. (2007) 'The Road from Oslo', *Disarmament Diplomacy* (85). Available at: www.acronym.org.uk/dd/dd85/85olso.htm. Date last accessed: April, 10 2011.

24. Russia (2005) 'Real or Mythical Threat', Presentation to the Group of Government Experts of States Parties to the Convention on Prohibitions or Restrictions on the Use of Certain Conventional Weapons Which May Be Deemed to Be Excessively Injurious or to Have Indiscriminate Effects, August.

25. As set out in Cohen, W. (2001) *Memorandum for the Secretaries of the Military Departments: Department of Defense Policy on Submunition Reliability*, January 10 (Washington, DC: Department of Defense).

26. Brazil (2005) *Response to Document CCW/GGE/X/WG.1/WP.2, Entitled IHL and ERW, dated 8 March 2005*, Group of Government Experts of States Parties to the Convention on Prohibitions or Restrictions on the Use of Certain Conventional Weapons Which May Be Deemed to Be Excessively Injurious or to Have Indiscriminate Effects CCW/GGE/XII/WG.1/WP.1, September 12; and United Kingdom (2005) *Responses to Document CCW/GGE/XI/WG.1/WP.2, Entitled IHL and ERW, dated 8 March 2005*, Group of Government Experts of States Parties to the Convention on Prohibitions or Restrictions on the Use of Certain Conventional Weapons Which May Be Deemed to Be Excessively Injurious or to Have Indiscriminate Effects CCW/GGE/XI/WG.1/WP.1, June 24.

27. Switzerland (2005) *Responses to Document CCW/GGE/X/WG.1/WP.2, entitled IHL and ERW, Dated 8 March 2005*, Group of Government Experts of States Parties to the Convention on Prohibitions or Restrictions on the Use of Certain Conventional Weapons Which May Be Deemed to Be Excessively Injurious or to Have Indiscriminate Effects CCW/GGE/XI/WG.1/WP.13, August 3; Ireland (2006) *Statement by Ireland to the Group of Governmental Experts of the CCW*, March 9; New Zealand (2006) *Statement by New Zealand to the Group of Governmental Experts of the CCW*, June 22; Norway (2006) *Responses to Document CCW/GGE/X/WG.1/WP.2, entitled IHL and ERW, Dated 8 March 2005* CCW/GGE/XI/WG.1/WP.5, July 29.

28. Greenwood QC, C. (2002) *Legal Issues Regarding Explosive Remnants of War*, Group of Government Experts of States Parties to the Convention on Prohibitions or Restrictions on the Use of Certain Conventional Weapons Which May Be Deemed to Be Excessively Injurious or to Have Indiscriminate Effects CCW/GGE/I/WP.10, May 23: 8.

29. For a detailed discussion see Rappert, B. and R. Moyes (2006) *Failure to Protect* (London: Landmine Action).

30. See Austria (2005) *Responses to Document CCW/GGE/XI/WG.1/WP.2, Entitled IHL and ERW, dated 8 March 2005*, Group of Government Experts of States Parties to the Convention on Prohibitions or Restrictions on the Use of Certain Conventional Weapons Which May Be Deemed to Be Excessively Injurious or to Have Indiscriminate Effects CCW/GGE/XI/WG.1/WP.14, August 4: 3; Norway (2005) *Responses to Document CCW/GGE/XI/WG.1/WP.2, Entitled IHL and ERW, dated 8 March 2005*, Group of Government Experts of States Parties to the Convention on Prohibitions or Restrictions on the Use of Certain Conventional Weapons Which May Be Deemed to Be Excessively Injurious or to Have Indiscriminate Effects CCW/GGE/XI/WG.1/WP.5, July 29: 5; Sweden (2005) *Responses to Document CCW/GGE/XI/WG.1/WP.2, Entitled IHL and ERW, dated 8 March 2005*, Group of Government Experts of States Parties to the Convention on Prohibitions or Restrictions on the Use

of Certain Conventional Weapons Which May Be Deemed to Be Excessively Injurious or to Have Indiscriminate Effects CCW/GGE/XI/WG.1/WP.8, July 29: 2; Hulme, K. (2005) 'Of Questionable Legality', *Canadian Yearbook of International Law* (December); McCormack, T. and P. Mtharu (2006) *Expected Civilian Damage and the Proportionality Equation*, Third Review Conference of the States Parties to the CCW CCW/CONF.III/WP.9, November 15.

31. Though not all did. For a detailed analysis see Rappert, B. and R. Moyes (2009) 'The Prohibition of Cluster Munitions: Setting International Precedents for Defining Inhumanity', Non-proliferation Review 16(2): 237–56.

32. Greenwood QC, C. (2002) *Legal Issues Regarding Explosive Remnants of War*, Group of Government Experts of States Parties to the Convention on Prohibitions or Restrictions on the Use of Certain Conventional Weapons Which May Be Deemed to Be Excessively Injurious or to Have Indiscriminate Effects CCW/GGE/I/WP.10, May 23: 8.

33. Herthel, Major T. (2001) 'On the Chopping Block: Cluster Munitions and the Law of War' *Air Force Law Review* (51): 256–9.

34. Garraway, C. (2005) 'How does Existing International Law Address the Issue of Explosive Remnants of War?' Twelfth Session of the Group of Governmental Experts of the States Parties to the CCW 17, November 17; McDonnell, T.M. (2002) 'Cluster Bombs Over Kosovo' *Arizona Law Review* 44: 34.

35. Hoon, G. (2000) *Evidence to House of Commons Select Committee on Defence*, June 21 (London: HMSO): Questions 121–6.

36. See also US/UK, Conduct of the 2003 War in Iraq, Case No. 153: 1600-0-1. Available at: https://portfolio.du.edu/portfolio/getportfoliofile?uid=82266. Date last accessed: March 23, 2011.

37. Hoon, G. (2003) *House of Commons Hansard*, April 7 (London: HMSO): Column 29; For similar statements justifying the appropriateness of cluster munitions see Hoon, G. (2003) *House of Commons Hansard*, April 14 (London: HMSO): Column 571W. See also Bach, W. (2001) *House of Lords Hansard*, November 21 (London: HMSO): Column WA141; and Bradshaw, B. (2003) *House of Commons Hansard*, March 27 (London: HMSO): Column 454.

38. Wiebe, V. (2008) 'For Whom the Little Bells Toll: Recent Judgments by International Tribunals on the Legality of Cluster Munitions', *Pepperdine Law Review* 35: 895–965.

39. Defense Science Board (2005) *Munitions System Reliability* (Washington, DC: Office of Under Secretary of Defense for Acquisition, Technology and Logistics): 2.

40. See, for example, Department of Defence (1999) *DoD News Briefing* 13 May Available at: www.defenselink.mil/transcripts/1999/t05131999_t0513asd.html. Date last accessed: March 23, 2011; and Department of Defense (2003) *DoD News Briefing Secretary Rumsfeld and Gen. Myers*, April 21.

41. On the program, see Hampson, F. (2010) 'The Principle of Proportionality in the Law of Armed Conflict', in S. Perrigo and J. Whitman (eds.) *The Geneva Conventions Under Assault* (London: Pluto): 53.

42. Rappert, B. (2005) *Out of Balance* (London: Landmine Action).

43. Russell, B. (2005) 'UK's Deadly Legacy: The Cluster Bomb' *The Independent*, November 21. Available at: www.independent.co.uk/news/uk/politics/uks-deadly-legacy-the-cluster-bomb-516229.html. Date last accessed: March 23, 2011.

44. Though on the back of this questioning it was argued that the UK consistently manipulated statistics to conform to official failure rates, see Moyes R. (2006) 'Failure Rates and the Protection of Civilians', *Landmine Action: Campaign*, Issue 12 (London: Landmine Action).

45. Compare, for instance, Ingram, A. (2004) 'Iraq', *House of Commons Hansard*, May 12 (London: HMSO): Column 328W; Ingram, A. (2003) 'Iraq', *House of Commons Hansard*, July 15 (London: HMSO): Column 192W; Ingram, A. (2004) 'Iraq', *House of Commons Hansard*, June 10 (London: HMSO): Column 605W.

46. It was not just the humanitarian side of the 'balance' sought under IHL that came into question during this time. Discord was voiced that the said military utility of cluster munitions rested on largely abstract arguments; this in contrast with growing documentation of humanitarian harms. See ICRC (2007) *Report of Expert Meeting – 'Humanitarian, Military, Technical and Legal Challenges of Cluster Munitions'* (Montreux), April 18–20: 30. On utility, see Geneva International Centre for Humanitarian Demining (2007) *A Guide to Cluster Munitions*, November (Geneva: GICHD): 27. For past examples of articulations of utility, see Germany (2004) *Reliability, Safety, and Performance of Conventional Munitions and Submunition*, Group of Government Experts of States Parties to the Convention on Prohibitions or Restrictions on the Use of Certain Conventional Weapons Which May Be Deemed to Be Excessively Injurious or to Have Indiscriminate Effects CCW/GGE/XI/WG.1/WP.2, November 29; and Paulsen, Major D. (2005) *Military Aspects of Ground Launched Cluster Munitions*, Group of Government Experts of States Parties to the Convention on Prohibitions or Restrictions on the Use of Certain Conventional Weapons Which May Be Deemed to Be Excessively Injurious or to Have Indiscriminate Effects, August.

47. Rappert, B. (2009) *Experimental Secrets* (Plymouth: University Press of America): Part III.

48. Rappert, B. (2005) *Out of Balance: The UK Government's Efforts to Understand Cluster Munitions and International Humanitarian Law* (London: LandmineAction).

49. Green, P. and T. Ward. (2004) *State Crime* (London: Pluto): 3.

50. Jochnick, C. and R. Normand (1994) 'The Legitimation of Violence: A Critical History of the Laws of War', *Harvard International Law Journal* 35(1): 49.

51. Redding, Paddy (2006) Correspondence to Richard Moyes Regarding FoI Request, November 13.

52. See (2001) 'Cluster Bombs', *House of Commons Hansard*, November 5 (London: HMSO): Column 1W.

53. Johnson, P.C. (2002) *Secrets, Gossip and Gods* (Oxford: Oxford University Press): 3. Emphasis taken out of the original.

54. For a discussion of this see Gunn, J. (2005) *Modern Occult Rhetoric* (Tuscaloosa: University of Alabama Press).

55. Greenwood, C. (2002) *Legal Issues Regarding Explosive Remnants of War*, Group of Government Experts of States Parties to the Convention on Prohibitions or Restrictions on the Use of Certain Conventional Weapons Which May Be Deemed to Be Excessively Injurious or to Have Indiscriminate Effects CCW/GGE/I/WP.10, May 23: 8.

56. Major Thomas Herthel of the US Air Force Judge Advocate General School offered perhaps the most in-depth legal analysis that downplayed concern about

them. Many of its central claims were substantiated by appeals to the authority of commanders and information generally restricted to those outside the US military establishment. See Herthel, Major T. (2001) 'On the Chopping Block: Cluster Munitions and the Law of War', *Air Force Law Review* 51: 256–9. For examples of the use of hypothetical reasoning see Hampson, F. (2010) 'The Principle of Proportionality in the Law of Armed Conflict', in S. Perrigo and J. Whitman (eds.) *The Geneva Conventions under Assault* (London: Pluto).

57. The group included Austria, the Holy See, Ireland, Mexico, New Zealand, Norway, and Peru.

58. Article 2 in the final text of the CCM defined a cluster munition as meaning 'a conventional munition that is designed to disperse or release explosive submunitions each weighing less than 20 kilograms, and includes those explosive submunitions. It does not mean the following:

a. A munition or submunition designed to dispense flares, smoke, pyrotechnics or chaff; or a munition designed exclusively for an air defence role;
b. A munition or submunition designed to produce electrical or electronic effects;
c. A munition that, in order to avoid indiscriminate area effects and the risks posed by unexploded submunitions, has all of the following characteristics:
i. Each munition contains fewer than ten explosive submunitions;
ii. Each explosive submunition weighs more than four kilograms;
iii. Each explosive submunition is designed to detect and engage a single target object;
iv. Each explosive submunition is equipped with an electronic self-destruction mechanism;
v. Each explosive submunition is equipped with an electronic self-deactivating feature'.

59. Borrie, J. (2007) 'The road from Oslo', *Disarmament Diplomacy* 85. Available at: www.acronym.org.uk/dd/dd88/88jb.htm. Date last accessed: March 23, 2011 and Borrie, J. (2009) *Unacceptable Harm* (Geneva: United Nations).

60. Rappert, B. and R. Moyes (2009) 'The Prohibition of Cluster Munitions: Setting International Precedents for Defining Inhumanity', *Non-proliferation Review* 16(2): 237–56.

61. Bettauer, R. (2006) *Opening Statement by the United States to the 3rd Review Conference of the Convention on Certain Conventional Weapons 7 November*. Available at: http://geneva.usmission.gov/2006/11/07/opening-statement-nov07-2006/. Date last accessed: March 23, 2011.

62. Convention on Cluster Munitions (2007) 'Chair's Discussion Text for Vienna Conference', December 2007. Available at: www.clusterconvention.org/pages/pages_vi/vib_opdoc_chairsvienna.html. Date last accessed: September 15, 2011.

63. See Borrie, J. (2009) *Unacceptable Harm* (Geneva: United Nations): Chapter 7.

64. Dullum, O. (2007) *Cluster Weapons – Military Utility and Alternatives*, Report 2007/02345 (Kjeller: Norwegian Defence Research Establishment).

65. These states either focused on only one characteristic of weapons – their number of submunitions or reliability – or offered less demanding cumulative criteria. See *Compendium of Proposals Submitted by Delegations During the Wellington Conference- Addendum 1*. Available at: www.mfat.govt.nz/clustermunition-swellington/conference-documents/WCCM-Compendium-v2.pdf. Date last accessed: March 23, 2011.

66. Taken from Rappert, B. and R. Moyes (2010) 'Enhancing the Protection of Civilians from Armed Conflict: Precautionary Lessons', *Medicine, Conflict & Survival* 26(1): 33.

67. Just how important such argumentative absences were in the final settlement of the CCM is a matter open for debate. A comprehensive history of the Oslo Process maintained that the definition structure was vital in the convention securing the gains it did. See Borrie, J. (2009) *Unacceptable Harm* (Geneva: United Nations).

4   COVERT CONVERSATIONS AND PUBLIC SECRETS?: THE BANNING OF CLUSTER MUNITIONS

1. One that also makes use of previous correspondence, notably an email exchange between Brian Rappert and Richard Moyes that was the basis for a paper presented to the 24th Colloquium of the European Group for Organizational Studies in July 2008.

2. Rappert, B. and R. Moyes (2009) 'The Prohibition of Cluster Munitions: Setting International Precedents for Defining Inhumanity', *Non-proliferation Review* 16(2): 237–56.

3. For an account with acknowledgement of the role of individuals see Borrie, J. (2009), *Unacceptable Harm* (Geneva: United Nations).

4. For a primer on skepticism as envisioned here read Grint, K. and S. Woolgar (1997) *The Machine at Work* (Cambridge: Polity).

5. See Rappert, B. and R. Moyes (2006) Failure to Protect (London: Landmine Action).

6. Rappert, B. (2005) *Out of Balance* (London: Landmine Action). Among the findings of this report were the conclusions that the UK had undertaken no practical assessments of the humanitarian impact of cluster munitions and does not gather information that would be useful to such assessments (such as the type, and country of origin, of submunitions found during disposal operations) despite being in a position to do so.

7. Rappert, B. and R. Moyes (2006) Failure to Protect (London: Landmine Action).

8. Professor Ken Rutherford from Missouri State University and the NGO Survivor Corps.

9. Austria passed comprehensive legislation prohibited cluster munitions in December 2007.

10. This matter was not resolved in November 2010 when Wikileaks released an American diplomatic record of a US–UK non-proliferation meeting wherein the British diplomat Mariot Leslie was reported to have said that 'the UK was participating in both the CCW and Oslo Process as a "tactical maneuver" designed to keep activity within the bounds of [its] "redlines" and at the same time, keep the CCW alive'. See Secret Section 01 of 04 Paris 000245 –February 12, 2008. Available at: www.guardian.co.uk/world/us-embassy-cables-documents/140962. Date last accessed: March 23, 2011. To take that cable as revealing some underlying intent assumes, among other things, that it would be appropriate to attribute intent to 'the UK' overall, that Mariot Leslie was in possession of it, and that she spoke openly and honestly with the US about it. In short, it would be necessary to sideline the infighting, uncertainty, and deliberate deception that often characterizes diplomacy.

11. Available at: http://lm.icbl.org/index.php/publications/display?url=cm/2009/. Date last accessed: March 23, 2011.
12. For example, Committee of the Whole (2008) *Summary Record of the Eleventh Session of the Committee of the Whole CCM/CW/SR/11*, May 26.
13. In February 2010, the CCM obtained the required number of ratifications for it to enter into force.
14. As in Di Ruzza, T. (2009) 'The Convention on Cluster Munitions: Towards a Balance Between Humanitarian and Military Considerations?', *Military Law and the Law Of War Review* 47: 405–44; Kaldor, M. (2009) 'Dismantling the Global Nuclear Infrastructure', *openDemocracy.net*, August 12. Available at: www.isn.ethz.ch/isn/Current-Affairs/Security-Watch/Detail/?ots591=4888CAA0-B3DB-1461-98B9-E20E7B9C13D4&lng=en&id=104430. Date last accessed: March 23, 2011; and Cluster Munition Coalition (2011) 'US Led Attempt to Allow Cluster Bomb Use is Rejected at UN Negotiations', Press Release November 25.
15. In contrast to the way international diplomacy is often portrayed, as in Roberts, A. (2004) 'A Partial Revolution: The Diplomatic Ethos and Transparency in Intergovernmental Organizations', *Public Administration Review*, 64(4): 410–24.
16. See De Jong, F. (2007) *Masquerades of Modernity* (Edinburgh: Edinburgh University Press): 186.
17. Johnson, P.C. (2002) *Secrets, Gossip and Gods* (Oxford: Oxford University Press): 4.
18. Taking inspiration from Stocking, H. and L. Holstein (1993) 'Constructing and Reconstructing Scientific Ignorance', *Science Communication* 15(2): 186–210.
19. See Michaels, D. (2008) 'Manufactured Uncertainty' in R. Proctor and L. Schiebinger (eds.) *Agnotology* (Stanford, CA: Stanford University Press).
20. Smithson, M. (1989) *Ignorance and Uncertainty* (New York: Springer-Verlag).
21. As such, the conversation can be regarded as raising its own issues of trust associated with telling secrets. Trust is often at stake in the telling of secrets. In everyday life the telling of secrets is often prefaced by the disclaimer that the information is not to be shared, even though that is just what the teller does (Bellmen, B. (1981) 'The Paradox of Secrecy', *Human Studies* 4: 1–24). In this chapter the tension is not that what is disclosed should not be shared, but rather that what has been told is not all there is to tell but the account should be trusted.
22. Sparkes, A. (2000) 'Autoethnography and Narratives of Self', *Sociology of Sport Journal*, 17: 21–43.

5 BINDING OPTIONS

1. Buchanan, A. (2010) *Human Rights, Legitimacy, and the Use of Force* (Oxford: Oxford University Press).
2. Christensen, L.T. and R. Langer (2009) 'Public Relations and the Strategic Use of Transparency' in R.L. Heath, E. Toth and D. Waymer (eds.) *Rhetorical and Critical Approaches to Public Relations II* (London: Routledge): 129–53.
3. FCO (2010) *Freedom of Information Request: REF 1087-09*, January 7.
4. In its own way, Chapter 4 provided an instance of the way in which disclosure and concealment can mix in complex ways. While it sought to discuss what is not discussed, the production and text was also highly managed.

5. United Nations Development Programme and World Health Organization (2005) *The Global Armed Violence Prevention Programme (AVPP) – Phase I Programme*, Document June 2; United Nations – Secretary-General (2005) in *Larger Freedom: Towards Development, Security and Human Rights for All*, March 21, A/59/2005; OECD Development Assistance Committee (2008) *Guidance on Armed Violence Reduction and Development* (Paris: OECD); Small Arm Survey (2008) *Small Arms Survey 2008: Risks and Resilience* (Cambridge: Cambridge University Press).

6. Geneva Declaration Secretariat (2008) *Global Burden of Armed Violence* (Geneva: Geneva Declaration Secretariat): 8.

7. Action On Armed Violence, Afghanistan Rights Monitor, Campaign for Innocent Victims in Conflict, Conflict Analysis Resource Center, Documenta, Croatia, Guatemalan Forensic Anthropology Foundation, Human Relief Foundation, Human Rights Center, Human Rights Watch, Iraq Body Count, NamRights, NATO Watch, Oxford Research Group, Research and Documentation Center, Somali Human Rights Association (2011) Libya: NGOs call on UN to record every casualty of conflict in Libya – Press Release, April 18.

8. Geneva Declaration Secretariat (2008) *Armed Violence Prevention and Reduction: A Challenge for Achieving the Millennium Development Goals*, June (Geneva: Geneva Declaration Secretariat).

9. See Rogers, P. (2011) 'The Casualties of War: Libya and Beyond', *openDemocracy*, July 7. Available at: www.opendemocracy.net/paul-rogers/casualties-of-war-libya-and-beyond.

10. UN Human Rights Council (2012) *Report of the International Commission of Inquiry on Libya* A/HRC/19/68 (Geneva: UN Human Rights Council).

11. Chivers, C.J. and E. Schmitt (2011) 'In Strikes on Libya by NATO, an Unspoken Civilian Toll', *New York Times*, December 17.

12. While the UK has signed the *Declaration*, at the time of writing the US has not.

13. Scarry, E. (1985) *The Body in Pain: The Making and Unmaking of the World* (Oxford: Oxford Paperbacks).

14. Demeritt, D. (2006) 'Science Studies, Climate Change and the Prospects for Constructivist Critique', *Economy and Society*, 35(3): 453–79.

15. See, for instance, Badkhen, A. (2006) 'Critics Say 600,000 Iraqi Dead Doesn't Tally. But Pollsters Defend Methods Used in Johns Hopkins Study', *San Francisco Chronicle*, October 12; Bird, S. (2004) 'Military and Public-health Sciences Need to Ally', *The Lancet* 364(9448): 1831–3; Cockburn, A. (2008) 'How the *New England Journal of Medicine* Undercounted Iraqi Civilian Deaths', *Counterpunch* (January 12/13); Morely, J. (2004) 'Is Iraq's Civilian Death Toll "horrible" – Or Worse?', *The Washington Post*, October 19.

16. See, for instance, Daponte, B.O. (2007) 'Wartime Estimates of Iraqi Civilian Casualties', *International Review of the Red Cross* 89(868): 943–57; Brownstein, C. and J. Brownstein (2008) 'Estimating Excess Mortality in Post-invasion Iraq', *New England Journal of Medicine* 358(5): 445–7; and Sloboda, J. (2009) *The Need to Acquire Accurate Casualty Records in Nato Operations* (Oxford: Oxford Research Group).

17. On this last question see Halimovic, D. (2008) 'Bosnian Researcher Counts War Dead, and Faces Threats for His Methods', *Radio Free Europe*, November 21. Available at: www.rferl.org/content/Bosnian_Researcher_Counts_The_Dead_And_Faces_Threats_For_His_Objectivity/1350799.html. Date last accessed: March 23, 2011.

18. See Cockburn, A. (2008) 'How the *New England Journal of Medicine* Undercounted Iraqi Civilian Deaths', *Counterpunch*, January 12/13. Contrast and compare the detail given in BBC (2008) 'New Study Says 151,000 Iraqi Dead', *BBC News*, January 10. Available at: http://news.bbc.co.uk/1/hi/world/middle_east/7180055.stm. Date last accessed: March 23, 2011; Steele, J. and S. Goldenberg (2008) 'What is the Real Death Toll in Iraq?', *The Guardian*, March 19. Available at: www.guardian.co.uk/world/2008/mar/19/iraq. Date last accessed: March 23, 2011; Associated Press (2010) 'U.S. Military Tallies Deaths of Iraqi Civilians and Forces', *New York Times*, October 14. Available at: www.nytimes.com/2010/10/15/world/middleeast/15iraq.html. Date last accessed: March 23, 2011; McArdle, M. (2008) 'Body Counting', *Atlantic Monthly*, April. Available at: www.theatlantic.com/magazine/archive/2008/04/body-counting/6698/; Hider, J. (2012) 'Cost of Toppling Saddam Hussein: 162,000 Dead', *The Times*, January 4. Available at: www.theaustralian.com.au/news/world/cost-of-toppling-saddam-hussein-162000-dead/story-e6frg6so-1226235912065. Date last accessed: January 4, 2012 and Rockel, S. (2009) 'Collateral Damage', in S. Rockel and R. Halpern (eds.) *Inventing Collateral Damage* (Toronto: Between the Lines): 64.
19. As in Ellis, M. (2009) 'Vital statistics', Professional Geographer 61(3): 301–9.
20. Contrast, for instance, Reynolds, P. (2010) 'Wikileaks: Iraq War Logs Increase Pressure for Openness', BBC News, October 27. Available at: www.bbc.co.uk/news/world-middle-east-11613349. Date last accessed: March 23, 2011; Leigh, D. (2010) 'Iraq War Logs Reveal 15,000 Previously Unlisted Civilian deaths', The Guardian, October 22. BBC News (2010) 'Violent Deaths in Iraq Fall "But at Slower Rate"', BBC News, December 30. Available at: www.bbc.co.uk/news/world-middle-east-12091385. Date last accessed: March 23, 2011.
21. Best, J. (2005) *The Limits of Transparency* (London: Cornell University Press): Chapter 1.
22. Press Release: *New Initiative on Recording Casualties of Armed Violence* 15 September 2011: 1.
23. As called for in the *Charter for the Recognition of Every Casualty of Armed Conflict*.
24. See, for instance, Ellis, M. (2009) 'Vital Statistics', Professional Geographer 61(3): 301–9 and Horton, R. (2007) 'A Monstrous War Crime', *The Guardian*, March 28.
25. See Maslen, S. and V. Wiebe (2008) *Cluster Munitions: A Survey of Legal Responses* (London: Landmine Action).
26. Whitaker, Q. (2008) 'Forward' in *Cluster Munitions: A Survey of Legal Responses* (London: Landmine Action).
27. Schmitt, M. (2010) 'Military Necessity and Humanity in International Humanitarian Law: Preserving the Delicate Balance', *Virginia Journal of International Law* 50(4): 838.
28. See Moyes, R. (2009) *Explosive Violence: The Problem of Explosive Weapons* (London: Landmine Action); and Rappert, B. and R. Moyes2010. 'Enhancing the Protection of Civilians from Armed Conflict: Precautionary Lessons', *Medicine, Conflict & Survival* 26(1): 24–47
29. Moritán, R.G. (2011) *Arm Trade Treaty Draft Paper*, July 14: 6.
30. van Zwanenberg, P. and A. Stirling (2004) 'Risk and Precaution in the US and Europe', *Yearbook of European Environmental Law* 3: 43–57.

31. Stern, J. and J. Wiener (2006) 'Precaution Against Terrorism', *Journal of Risk Research* 9(4): 393–447.
32. Smith, T. (2002) 'The New Law of War: Legitimizing Hi-tech and Infrastructural Violence', *International Studies Quarterly* 46: 355–74.
33. See also Sandoz Y. (1995) 'Preface' in E. Prokosch, *The Technology of Killing* (London: Zed).
34. Tannenwald, N. (1999) 'The Nuclear Taboo', *International Organization* 53(3): 436.
35. Eyre, D. and M. Schuman (1996) 'Status, Norms and the Proliferation of Chemical Weapons', in Peter Katzenstein (ed.) *The Culture of National Security* (New York: Columbia University Press).
36. Likewise, it has been argued that the growth after the Cold War in multilateral humanitarian interventions cannot be accounted for through traditional appeals to the pursuit of national power or material interest. See Finnemore, M. (1996) 'Constructing Norms of Humanitarian Intervention' in P. Katzenstein (ed.) *The Culture of National Security* (New York: Columbia University Press): 153–85; and Finnemore, M. (1996) *National Interests and International Security* (Ithaca: NY: Cornell University Press).
37. As in, for example, Price, R. (1998) 'Reversing the Gun Sights: Transnational Civil Society Targets Land Mines', *International Organization* 52 (Summer); and Brinkert, K. and K. Hamilton (2004) 'Clearing the Path to a Mine-free World' in R. Matthew, B. McDonald and K. Rutherford (eds.) *Landmines and Human Security* (Albany, NY: State University of New York Press).
38. Herby, P. and Lawand, K. (2008) 'Establishing Norms' in J. Williams, S. Goose and M. Wareham (eds.) *Banning Landmines* (London: Rowman and Littlefield).
39. Ibid.
40. See SIPRI (1971) *The Problem of Chemical Biological Warfare*, Volume 4 (Stockholm: Almqvist and Wiksell).
41. Despite the possibility of defensive protections that were not so readily available for many other force options.
42. Jenkins, D. (2002) *The Final Frontier: America, Science and Terror* (London: Verso).
43. Price, R. (1997) *The Chemical Weapons Taboo* (Ithaca, NY: Cornell University Press).
44. Price, R. and N. Tannenwald (1996) 'Norms and Deterrence' in P. Katzenstein (ed.) *The Culture of National Security* (New York: Columbia University Press): Chapter 5.
45. Dando, M. (1996) *A New Form of Warfare* (London: Brasseys): Chapter 3.
46. For a historical analysis of debates about the abhorrence of chemical weapons see Price, R. (1997) *The Chemical Weapons Taboo* (Ithaca, NY: Cornell University Press).
47. Keck, M. and K. Sikkink (1998) *Activists Beyond Borders* (Ithaca, NY: Cornell University Press): 34.
48. Kowert, P. and J. Legro (1996) 'Norms, Identity and their Limits', in P. Katzenstein (ed.) *The Culture of National Security* (New York: Columbia University Press).
49. See claims to this effect as well in Finnemore, M. and K. Sikkink (1998) 'International Norms Dynamics and Political Change', *International Organization* 52(4): 887–917; and Shannon, V. (2000) 'Norms are what States Make of Them', *International Studies Quarterly* 44: 293–316.

50. Payne, R. (2001) 'Persuasion, Frames and Norm Construction', *European Journal of International Relations* 7(1): 37–61.

51. Risse, T. (2002) 'Constructivism and International Institutions' in I. Katznelson and H. Milner (eds.) *Political Science* (London: WW Norton & Company, 2002): 597–623.

52. In this regard it can be noted that in providing no exemptions from the ban for 'acceptable cluster munitions' but only allowing exclusions for those technologies that are not considered to be 'cluster munitions', the CCM provides the sort of clear distinction needed for separating this category of weaponry from others and therefore stigmatizing it.

53. For a more lengthy discussion of what Tannenwald calls the 'permissive' effects of the nuclear taboo see Tannenwald, N. (2007) *The Nuclear Taboo* (Cambridge: Cambridge University Press): 317–24.

54. For an in-depth discussion of these issues see Pearson, A., M. Chevrier and M. Wheelis (eds.) (2007) Incapacitating Biochemical Weapons (Landham, MD: Lexington Press).

55. Falk, R. (2001) 'The Challenges of Biological Weaponry' in S. Wright (ed.) *Biological Warfare and Disarmament* (London: Rowman & Littlefield): 29.

6   FRAMING AND FRAMED: THE CATEGORY OF EXPLOSIVE VIOLENCE

1. For a classical treatment of frames see Goffman, E. (1974) *Frame Analysis: An Essay on the Organization of Experience* (New York, NY: Harper & Row).

2. Reese, S.D., O.H. Gandy Jr. and A.E. Grant (2001) *Framing Public Life* (Mahwah, NJ: Erlbaum): 6.

3. Gamson, W. and A. Modigliani (1989) 'Media Discourse and Public Opinion on Nuclear Power', *American Journal of Sociology* 95(1): 3.

4. McGill, A. (1997) 'Responsibility Judgments and the Causal Background', in D. Messick and A. Tenbrunsel (eds.) *Codes of Conduct* (New York: Russell Sage Foundation): 240.

5. Sasson, T. (1995) *Crime Talk: How Citizens Construct a Social Problem* (New York: Aldine De Gruyter).

6. See D'Angelo, P. and J. Kuypers 'Introduction' in P. D'Angelo and J. Kuypers (eds.) *Doing News Framing Analysis* (London: Routledge): 4.

7. Benford, R.D. and D.A. Snow (2000) 'Framing Processes and Social Movements', *Annual Review of Sociology* 26: 11–39; Gamson, W. and A. Modigliania (1989) 'Media Discourse and Public Opinion on Nuclear Power', *American Journal of Sociology* 95(1): 1–37; and Snow, D.A. and R.D. Benford (1988) 'Ideology, Frame Resonance and Participant Mobilization', *International Social Movement Research* 1: 197–219.

8. See Jasperson, A. and M. El-Kikhia (2003) 'CNN and Al Jazeera's Media Coverage of America's War in Afghanistan' in P. Norris, M. Kern, and M. Just (eds.) *Framing Terrorism* (London: Routledge).

9. See Rappert, B. (2006) *Controlling the Weapons of War: Politics, Persuasion and the Prohibition of Inhumanity* (London: Routledge).

10. Moyes, R. (2009) *Explosive Violence, The Problem of Explosive Weapons* (London: Landmine Action): 7. See as well UNIDR (2010) *Explosive Weapons: Framing the Problem*, April (Geneva: UNIDIR).

11. Moyes, R. (2009) *Explosive Violence, The Problem of Explosive Weapons* (London: Landmine Action): Chapter 1.
12. Defined for the purpose of this publication as 'any concentration of civilians, be it permanent or temporary, such as in inhabited parts of cities, or inhabited towns or villages, or as in camps or columns of refugees or evacuees, or groups of nomads', as in Protocol III of the 1980 Convention on Certain Conventional Weapons.
13. See Boer, R., B. Schuurman and M. Struyk (2011) *Protecting Civilians from Explosive Weapons* (Utrecht: Pax Christi Netherlands); and Smith, K. (2011) *Devastating Impact: Explosive Weapons and Children* (London: Save the Children UK).
14. UN Security Council (2009) *Report of the Secretary-General on the Protection of Civilians in Armed Conflict* S/2009/277, May 29: Paragraph 36.
15. Statement by John Holmes, Under-Secretary-General for Humanitarian Affairs and Emergency Relief Coordinator (2010) *Security Council Open Debate on the Protection of Civilians in Armed Conflict*, July 7.
16. UN Emergency Relief Coordinator (2011) *United Nations Humanitarian Chief Highlights Humanitarian Consequences of Continued Fighting in Libya*, March 17 (New York: OCHA).
17. UN Emergency Relief Coordinator (2011) *United Nations Humanitarian Chief Alarmed at Cote D'Ivoire Violence*, March 18 (New York: OCHA).
18. Human Rights Watch (2011) 'Libya: Government Lays More Mines in Western Mountains', July 8. Press release available at: www.hrw.org/news/2011/07/08/libya-government-lays-more-mines-western-mountains; and Human Rights Watch (2011) 'Libya: Cluster Munitions Strike Misrata', April 15. Press release available at: www.hrw.org/fr/news/2011/04/15/libya-cluster-munitions-strike-misrata.
19. International Committee of the Red Cross (2011) *Healthcare in Danger*, July (Geneva: ICRC).
20. For a discussion of media portrayals of events involving explosive weapons, see Brehm, M. (2010) 'Explosive Weapons Use in Somalia and the International Response to It', presentation to the conference 'Explosive Weapons and Civilians: Framing the Problem', April 29, 2010 (Geneva). Available at: www.unidir.org/bdd/fiche-activite.php?ref_activite=527. Date last accessed: April 13, 2011.
21. For a discussion of episodic and thematic framing, and in particular what they mean for notions of responsibility, see Iyengar, S. (1991) *Is Anyone Responsible?* (London: University of Chicago Press).
22. For a wider development of this argument see Moyes, R. (2009) *Explosive Violence, The Problem of Explosive Weapons* (London: Landmine Action).
23. Smith, R. (2005) *The Utility of Force: The Art of War in the Modern World* (London: Allen Lane).
24. For a discussion of technological fixes in relation to explosive weapons see UNIDIR (2010) *Use of Explosive Weapons in Populated Areas: Some Questions and Answers*, July (Geneva: UNIDIR).
25. US Marine Corps (1998) *Joint Concept for Non-Lethal Weapons* (Quantico, VA: US Marine Corps).
26. See Davison, N. (2009) *'Non-Lethal' Weapons* (London: Palgrave Macmillan); Amnesty International USA (2004) *Excessive and Lethal Force? Amnesty International's Concerns about Deaths and Ill-treatment Involving Police Use of*

Tasers, Report No. AMR 51/139/2004 (New York: Amnesty International); Altmann, J., (2001) 'Acoustic Weapons: A Prospective Assessment', *Science & Global Security* 9: 165–234; and Rappert, B. (2003) *Non-Lethal Weapons as Legitimizing Forces?* (London: Frank Cass).

27. See Davison, N. (2009) *'Non-Lethal' Weapons* (London: Palgrave Macmillan).

28. See, for instance, Rappert, B. (2007) 'Policing & the Use of Force', Policing: A Journal of Policy and Practice 1(4): 472–84; and Rappert, B. (2002) 'Assessing Chemical Incapacitants', International Journal of Police Science and Management 4(2): 115–26.

29. For a recent illustration of the contest about labels in this area, see Casey-Maslen, S. (2010) *Non-kinetic-energy Weapons Termed 'Non-lethal': A Preliminary Assessment under International Humanitarian Law and International Human Rights Law*, October (Geneva: Geneva Academy of International Humanitarian Law and Human Rights).

30. One point of note here is that to the extent the problem is defined as owing to the context of the use of force (in populated areas), then what is being called into question is the possibility of armed conflict in populated areas in general. As such, attention to explosive weapons would be a way of drawing attention to the harms of conflict much more widely.

31. Snow, D.A. and R.D. Benford (1988) 'Ideology, Frame Resonance and Participant Mobilization', *International Social Movement Research* 1: 197–219.

32. International Committee of the Red Cross (2011) *International Humanitarian Law and the Challenges of Contemporary Armed Conflicts* 31IC/11/5.1.2 (Geneva: ICRC): 41. For another IHL framing example see Human Rights Watch and Harvard Law School International Human Rights Clinic (2011) *Documentation of the Use of Explosive Weapons in Populated Areas*, November (New York: HRW and IHRC).

33. As in Smith, K. (2011) *Devastating Impact: Explosive Weapons and Children* (London: Save the Children UK); Puente, H.E. (2010) *Statement by the Permanent Representative of Mexico to the United Nations*, Open Debate on the Protection of Civilians During Armed Conflict, November 22, 2010, Security Council Chamber (GA-TSC-01); and Schwaiger, P. (2010) *Statement by the Deputy Head of the Delegation of the European Union to the United Nations*, Open Debate on the Protection of Civilians During Armed Conflict, November 22, 2010, Security Council Chamber (GA-TSC-01).

34. Doswald-Beck, L. (2006) 'The Right to Life in Armed Conflict: Does International Humanitarian Law Provide All the Answers?' *International Review of the Red Cross* 88(864): 881–904 and Heintze, H.-J. (2004) 'On the Relationship Between Human Rights Law Protection and International Humanitarian Law', *International Review of the Red Cross* Vol. 86(856): 789–814.

35. As in Smith, K. (2011) *Devastating Impact: Explosive Weapons and Children* (London: Save the Children UK).

36. For a useful summary, see World Health Organization (2002) *World Report on Violence and Health* (Geneva: WHO).

37. Mercy, J.A., M.L. Rosenberg, K.E. Powell, C.V. Broome, and W.L. Roper (1993) 'Public Health Policy for Preventing Violence', *Health Affairs* 12(4): 7–29.

38. World Health Organization (2004) *Preventing Violence: A Guide to Implementing the Recommendations of the World Report on Violence and Health* (Geneva: WHO): 5–6.

39. Valenti, M., C.M. Ormhaug, R.E. Mtonga and J. Loretz (2007) 'Armed Violence: A Health Problem, a Public Health Approach', *Journal of Public Health Policy* 28(4): 389–400.

40. Small Arms Survey (2008) *Small Arms Survey 2008* (Oxford: Oxford University Press): Chapter 7.

41. Korn, D., R. Gibbins and J. Azmier (2003) 'Framing Public Policy Towards a Public Health Paradigm for Gambling', *Journal of Gambling Studies* 19(2): 235–56.

42. Here it is interesting to note that the Convention on Cluster Munitions contains obligations under Article 5 to 'collect reliable relevant data with respect to cluster munition victims'. Such an explicit obligation to collect data on victims of armed violence is novel within international arms treaties. Moreover, under the convention the definition of 'victims' covers conflict and post-conflict periods; applies to combatants and non-combatants; and covers physical and psychological harm to individuals as well as indirect social and economic deprivation to individuals, families and communities.

43. Needed information to be gathered would therefore include: the date; geographic location and context of incidents; details of the weapons used (at a minimum whether these were explosive weapons, firearms, etc.); the actors using these weapons; (notional) intended targets and people in the vicinity, and their level of vulnerability; the factors leading to deaths and injuries; demographic information on affected populations; and damage caused to property and other assets. On many of these points see Taback N. and Coupland, R. (2006) 'Security of Journalists: Making the Case for Modelling Armed Violence as a Means to Promote Human Security', in J. Borrie and V. Martin Randin (eds.) *Thinking Outside the Box in Multilateral Disarmament and Arms Control Negotiations* (Geneva: United Nations Institute for Disarmament Research).

44. See Amnesty International September (2011) *The Battle for Libya*, MDE 19/025/2011: 78; and Action on Armed Violence (2011) *Explosive Violence Report: 16–29 September 2011* (London: AOAV).

45. As part of this they could gather data on explosive weapon victims under their jurisdiction or control; provide assistance to victims (including medical care, rehabilitation, and psychological support); facilitate their social and economic inclusion; and ensure the rapid clearance of unexploded and abandoned weapons from territory over which they have jurisdiction or control.

46. United Nations Mine Action Service (2003) *Mine Action and Effective Coordination: The United Nations Policy*, May (Geneva: UN MAS).

47. Who is identified as suffering is tied to who speaks for suffering. As mentioned in the previous section, public-health framings should be open to contributions from many fields of study – epidemiology, education, ethics, sociology, economics, and psychology to name a few. Yet, as health-centered approaches, in practice just who speaks with what credibility under such framings is a potential source of concern. Given their experience and knowledge, medical and health professionals are well placed to provide a lead in such discussions. Whatever the appropriateness of such as 'leading' in the abstract, it can mean certain ways of thinking get marginalized – as has arguably taken place in some respects with regard to legalistic approaches to governing the conduct of war.

48. See report of a residential symposium co-hosted by UNIDIR's Discourse on Explosive Weapons (DEW) project and The Geneva Forum (Glion) 4–5 December 2010.

49. In the case of the Convention on Cluster Munitions, one of the ways the extent of attention on this topic could build a more comprehensive understanding of harm in conflict more generally is in the definitions and requirements it gives in relation to 'cluster munition victims'. The convention stipulates that data collection should be implemented without discrimination on the basis of the type of weapon that has caused victimization. See Rappert, B. and R. Moyes (2010) 'Enhancing the Protection of Civilians from Armed Conflict: Precautionary Lessons', *Medicine, Conflict & Survival* 26(1): 24–47.

50. As part of the potential never-ending unpacking that could be done in relation to what is framed and how, it would be possible to go further and question what attention suffering from conflict should receive in relation to other types of suffering.

51. My thanks to John Borrie and Maya Brehm for this point.

52. Nisbet, M. (2010) 'Knowledge into Action: Framing Debates over Climate Change and Poverty' in P. D'Angelo and J. Kuypers (eds.) *Doing News Framing Analysis* (London: Routledge): 43–83.

CONCLUSION: PULLING BACK

1. Lochrie, K. (1999) *Covert Operations: The Medieval Uses of Secrecy* (Philadelphia: University of Pennsylvania Press): 4.

2. Dewey, J. (1929) *The Quest for Certainty* (London: George Allen & Unwin).

3. As in Robertson, K.G. (1999) *Secrecy and Open Government* (London: Macmillan).

4. See Andreas, P. and K. Greenhill (2010) 'Introduction' in P. Andreas and K. Greenhill (eds.) *Sex, Drugs, and Body Counts* (London: Cornell University Press): 1–22; as well as Rogers, P. (2011) 'The Casualties of War: Libya and Beyond', openDemocracy, July 7. Available at: www.opendemocracy.net/paul-rogers/casualties-of-war-libya-and-beyond. Date last accessed: March 3, 2012.

5. Beale, J. (2011) 'Counting the Cost of Nato's Mission in Libya', *BBC News*, October 31. Available at: www.bbc.co.uk/news/world-africa-15528984. Date last accessed: October 31, 2011.

6. As in the case of Andreas, P. and K. Greenhill (2010) 'Conclusion: The Numbers in Politics' in P. Andreas and K. Greenhill (eds.) *Sex, Drugs, and Body Counts* (London: Cornell University Press): 264–78.

Index

Compiled by Sue Carlton